W9-BIC-552

Ten First Street, Southeast

CONGRESS BUILDS A LIBRARY, 1886–1897

An exhibition in the Great Hall and on the Second Floor
of the Thomas Jefferson Building
Library of Congress

Helen-Anne Hilker

Library of Congress   Washington   1980

Dedicated to David Chambers Mearns and to the memory
of Verner Warren Clapp, mentors and creative librarians

Library of Congress Cataloging in Publication Data

Hilker, Helen-Anne.
   Ten First Street, Southeast: Congress builds a
library, 1886–1897.

   Includes bibliographical references.
   Supt. of Docs. no.: LC 12:C76/9
   1. United States. Library of Congress.
Thomas Jefferson Building—History—Exhibitions.
I. United States. Library of Congress. II. Title.
Z679.2.U54H54   027.5753   80–607808
ISBN 0–8444–0351–2

FRONT COVER: *In this 1898 view from the heights of the United States Capitol, the Detroit Publishing Company captured the color of the erstwhile gold dome of the "new" Library building. Gilded in 1893, the dome was a spectacular feature of Capitol Hill for 38 years. In the 20th century weather and the chemical effects of the 19th-century method of tinning the copper beneath the gold leaf combined to produce perforations in the copper, and finally the leaking gilded copper was replaced in October 1931. By that time, it was thought that gold leaf would conflict with the appearance of the aging granite, and the new copper was left to acquire the patina now so familiar half a century later.*

TITLE PAGE: *Even this black-and-white photograph of the Library building shows the brilliance of the early gilded dome. The statue of George Washington in the foreground, which then sat on the east plaza of the U. S. Capitol, was moved early in the 20th century to the Smithsonian Institution. LC–USP6–6534–A*

For sale by the Superintendent of Documents, U.S. Government Printing Office, Washington, D.C. 20402

Contents

This article, originally published in the *Quarterly Journal of the Library of Congress* of October 1972 to mark the 75th anniversary of the Library of Congress 1897 building, has been revised and updated by the author.

On July 11, 1893, when this photographic record of progress in constructing the Library's new building was made for the engineers, the main pavilion at the center of the west front lacked its fourth story, and the windows for the Main Reading Room in the octagon of the rotunda directly behind the pavilion could still be seen. On the portico above the second story of this pavilion can be seen the eight empty granite bases that awaited the 16 pillars of 14,200 pounds each that were to be hoisted to the third level and set in place in the coming weeks. LC–USP6–6519–A

Monument to Civilization

DIARY OF A BUILDING

Architect John L. Smithmeyer (1832–1908)

Architect Paul J. Pelz (1841–1918)

When, in 1872, the Library of Congress collections had overflowed their quarters in the U.S. Capitol, Librarian Ainsworth Rand Spofford asked Congress for a separate building to house them and provide library services. Congress responded in 1873 by holding an architectural competition. This design, done in the style of the Italian Renaissance by architects Smithmeyer & Pelz, won first prize. Alternative designs by these two and by other architects were later considered for one location or another, as the exhibition indicates, until a refined version of this original Smithmeyer & Pelz design was accepted in 1886. The two architects made some changes in their design in the next two years, then delays in construction led to changes in personnel and to further changes in design. The plan by Paul J. Pelz to which Congress gave final approval early in 1889 also underwent alteration during construction, as viewers of the exhibition will note, and changes were made in the decorations. But the final structure evolved from this design and retained the style of the Italian Renaissance.

Monument to Civilization

DIARY OF A BUILDING

On Monday, July 24, 1893, the granite walls for the "new Library of Congress" were rising steadily on Capitol Hill.

Some 200 men were plying their various building trades on the 10½-acre site. In different parts of the Nation, another 300 were preparing iron or marble or brick or other components under contracts for the 3½-acre structure. The exterior walls at the building's perimeter were nearing the top of the third story above ground, and coppering on the dome over the central rotunda was well along.

Stonemasons were at work on the main portico facing west toward the Capitol. The morning paper had predicted "Dry, Very Dry," with rain "a long way off."

Civil Engineer Bernard R. Green, superintendent in immediate charge of construction, went to Baltimore that day. Nearly 50 and a native of New England, Mr. Green was a man of careful record. From October 1888 until nearly five years after this palace for the printed word was opened in 1897, he kept a diary of its creation. Thus it is known that his trip in the summer heat was made to inspect "progress and character of work on marble for the Main Stair Hall at Evans & Sons works. . . ." [1] He also inquired about gold leaf and methods of gilding the Library's dome.

After lunch, the stonemasons tried to reset the second column south of the portico's center. The shaft—19.7 feet tall, 2.4 feet in diameter, weighing 7.1 tons—was suspended about a foot above its base from a lewis inserted at the top. Mr. Green would later note in his journal, his chagrin evident, that the men had not placed the lug-band—"especially provided to resist the splitting action of the lewis"—around the top of the stone. Inspec-

tion would show that the lewis-hole had been defectively cut, but "the lug-band would have prevented rupture nevertheless had it been on and properly tightened." [2]

Around this sketch in his journal, Mr. Green wrote, "The hole for the lewis was thus . . . 7¼" deep." LC–USP6–6541–A

At about 1:20 P.M., the lewis burst from its hole. The stone dropped "plumb on its bed, smashing off the right hand of the mason Wm. Corcoran. . . ." [3]

The work went on. Gilders began on August 14 to lay the gold leaf Mr. Green had sought for the dome. Two weeks later, a new column and base, procured to replace those damaged in the accident, were set in place.

By mid-November, the golden dome was blinding in the sun. Plans for the artistic decoration of the building's interior were maturing that winter, and in January 1894 the upper section of the scaffold inside the rotunda beneath the dome was removed to make way for "the first of the Dome travelling scaffolds." [4] It was from one of these ingenious revolving scaffolds, which were designed by Mr. Green and tested on February 19, that the interior of the dome was coffered, ribbed, plastered, and filled with Albert Weinert's variegated figures in stucco relief by the end of the next January. Below, in the great octagonal rotunda, brick and marble and iron work continued throughout 1895.

A force of some 350 to 400 men—plus the workmen of contractors—now swarmed about all parts of the massive building. On Friday, September 13, 1895, no record was made of how many were in the octagon, which stretches 125 feet from dome to floor and 100 feet from side to side. The day was warm and humid. A waterboy for Snead & Co. Iron Works, accustomed to making his way about the scaffolds, was on an upper level. At the time—about 1:30 P.M.—no one was near enough to be sure what happened. Walter Acton, at 18 the "support of his widowed mother," apparently tripped near the hatch through which materials were hoisted. John Chambers, engineer in charge of Snead & Company's work, looked up from a lower scaffold to see a body hurtling through the rotunda. Young Acton plunged nearly 70 feet to the main floor. He was killed instantly.[5]

Again, the work went on, its pace unremitting.

The Men Who Built Her

William Corcoran gave his hand and Walter Acton his brief life toward the creation of this monument to civilization. Architects might quarrel over credit for its design and engineers take top billing on its marble tablet. Artists might hunger for commissions and critics scold about the choice of names memorialized in sculpture. In the long run of time, all—artists, architects, and engineers—would have their just due in the histories that would record their names for posterity.

But when the new creation towered on the horizon, she belonged equally to the anonymous men who built her with their hands, and they knew it. Their children knew it, their nieces and nephews knew it, and their grandchildren would know it, generation after generation. They still come to the Library, saying "My granddaddy—" or "My great-uncle—" or "My great-grandfather worked on this building. He was a stonecutter—" or "a bricklayer—" or "an ironworker."

There were carpenters and copperers, electricians and gilders. Glassmakers, hodcarriers, mortarers, mechanics. Pipefitters, plumbers, plasterers, painters. Riggers, steamfitters, tool-

Bernard Richardson Green (1843–1914), New Englander, Unitarian, Harvard man, Sunday school superintendent, trustee of a bank and an art gallery, member of scientific and artistic groups, lecturer, canoeist, choralist, and diarist. LC–USP6–6496–A

makers, woodworkers. And more. Some worked in quarries or factories far from Washington, some came to the Capital for a few weeks or months, still others lived here.

From March of 1889, when Congress passed the act approving the final plans and funds, until the building was occupied in 1897, construction work proceeded day after relentless day for eight years.

Managing all phases of construction nearly every working day of those eight years—and sometimes on Sunday—was the building's first documentalist, Bernard Richardson Green. Hired by the Commission for the Construction of the Congressional Library Building on March 19, 1888, when he came for an interview with its members at the request of the

Secretary of the Interior, he reported for duty on April 2.[6]

When Congress dispensed with the services of John L. Smithmeyer as architect on October 2 that year and placed Brig. Gen. Thomas Lincoln Casey (the Army's newly promoted chief of engineers) in charge, Bernard Green —a civilian—continued as superintendent of construction. Paul J. Pelz, assistant architect, became architect until April 1892. Late that year, the general's son replaced him. When General Casey died on March 25, 1896, scarcely a week elapsed before Congress passed a joint resolution promoting Mr. Green as successor in the building's overall direction.[7]

In the act of February 19, 1897, providing appropriations for the Library's operations in the new building and, more broadly, for its organization, custody, and management, Congress placed the care and maintenance of the building and its grounds in the separate custody of a superintendent, who, like the Librarian of Congress, would be appointed by the President, by and with the advice and consent of the Senate. And when President Cleveland sent the name of John Russell Young to the Senate on June 30, 1897, in nomination for the librarianship of Congress, the name of Bernard R. Green accompanied it in nomination as superintendent of the Library building and grounds.[8] He continued in that post until 1914, overseeing the move and the final decoration—the last artist left in 1902!—as well as the operation of the mechanized building.[9]

The Diarist

It was Bernard Green, therefore, who for 14 of his 26 years with the Library was in constant and intimate attendance on the work of the men whose hands created the building. It is he who lifts them and their labors from obscurity in his detailed records of the construction, decoration, furnishing, occupation, opening, and operation of a great library. Although he could record only a relatively few individual names, all their accomplishments and mishaps appear in his journal. And, besides the journal, he kept a remarkably revealing scrapbook of what the public prints had to say about the building, the Library, the work of the men.

For those who do not build but only marvel, these documents create an astonishing and overwhelming picture: a mosaic of all the components of men and materials and talents —and their ultimately successful meshing amid the problems—that are required to erect an architectural wonder of such magnitude and complexity, of such public and Congressional interest.

The two notebooks of Mr. Green's journal which are extant in the Library of Congress begin in October 1888, when he resumed an accustomed relationship of more than a decade with General Casey.[10] In 1877 the latter had been assigned to Washington with responsibility for public buildings and grounds. Then a colonel, he was placed in charge of the Washington aqueduct and the completion of the State, War, and Navy building (now the Executive Office Building) at 17th Street and Pennsylvania Avenue, N.W. In 1878 Colonel Casey was given the added job of completing the Washington Monument, and in 1885–86 he was in charge of constructing the Army Medical Museum and Library building.[11]

Colonel Casey directed and Mr. Green superintended the work on these construction projects. It was the simultaneous work on the two unfinished structures, however, that established their reputations. They built two wings and a central section (1878–88) of the State, War, and Navy building for $2 million less than the first two wings (1871–77) had cost under their predecessors; and the Washington Monument, begun 30 years before with a foundation inadequate for its mass, was hailed after they completed it (1879–84) as "one of the engineering marvels of this century." [12]

With that background, Mr. Green was confident of his experience and ability when he was interviewed by the Commission that day in March 1888. In the letter of summation which the members asked him to write as a record of his responses and observations during their meeting, he could say:

> I should state that I have never made application, even in the most indirect way, for the position in question, nor any other under the Commission, but that all motion in the matter has come from other quarters, and, to me, some unknown and unexpected ones.[13]

What kind of man was this letter-writer who had been sought by the Commission?

Glimpses of Bernard Green the person emerge from both scrapbook and journal between the records of the engineer and public man. They may be inaccurate; the man himself has vanished.

Pictures of a Man

His journal is nearly all business. Here are the brief notations of negotiations conducted, progress in the various stages of the work, setbacks suffered at times with patience but more often with frustration, pride when a hard job proved successful. The pronoun "I" rarely appears—most entries begin with a verb and refer to the work of all who were involved. Human affairs creep in among the brusque reports of facts, however. The inner viewpoint can be easily misconstrued, but the phrasing often seems revealing.

Recording the hoisting of ironwork sections into the crown of the dome on March 10, 1892, he says: "They only arrived this morning." When laborer William Sarner finds his trousers and 18 dollars stolen from the basement of the octagon on July 17, 1894, the diarist adds to his report: "his pay for ½ month."

On October 20, 1893, he complains to his journal of a contractor's delay: "This destroys plans for the winter's work in the W. M. and puts it all back 6 months, because they are already 3 months behind time, and hardly one half of that part of the marble work finished." [14] In 1895 he notes that on June 13

the wife of draftsman Winthrop Alexander died that morning, and on October 17 he writes: "Edward J. Sheehy, for many years our faithful janitor and messenger, died last night of cancer of the stomach."

He records death frequently. He reports every accident and the nature of the injuries, sometimes checking on the injuries the following day and noting the final report in the next entry. He does not make an entry for every single day—only for events worth noting.

The scrapbook casts light on both the inner and the public man, insofar as such a collection can, with its clippings on subjects that interested him in his reading of the popular press and those that relate directly to his own activities. The view the public had of him in the latter can be seen in the way newsmen reacted to his interviews, in the occasional remarks of Members of Congress in their *Record,* and in the statements he himself made to the press.[15]

The articles about his building projects contain many direct quotations. If they were recorded with reasonable accuracy—and nearly all ring with the tones, if not the brevity, of his journal entries—Mr. Green was an outspoken, no-nonsense man. Nor was he ever confused about the identification of spades.

If a proposition appeared ridiculous to him, he said so, and he said why. When he was queried in December 1896 about what he dubbed "an idle rumor" that the 1897 inaugural ball might be held in the new and unoccupied Library building, he told the reporter in terms that no inaugural committee could misunderstand: "I am opposed to the use of the building for this purpose." Why? "The beauty and delicacy of the decorations, the mural paintings, the carving in marble and onyx, enhance the chances for accidental damage, while the foolish curiosity that insists on poking and picking to see what things are made of would undoubtedly be in evidence in such a gathering." And there was more—six inches more of direct quotation.[16]

properly tightened. The hole for the lewis was thus, [drawing] 7¼" deep.

July 25.
Bronze deck of lantern.

Began laying the bronze deck of lantern gallery on the dome.

August 1.
Copper finish of Dome.

Began putting up the copper cornice work at base of dome, — being the beginning of the ornamental work on the dome.

Cementing on dome.

— Finished cementing upper surface of dome.

Stonework.

— Resumed stone setting on N. E. P. — Second story, the few stones wanted having come within a few days past. Set the last of the B stones, — column pedestals on north face.

Aug. 3.
Marble work.

Contractors (Batterson, See & Eisele) began setting the marble work of Reading Room.

Aug. 9.
Key Plans to Mr. Spofford.

Sent to Mr. Spofford, Librarian, a set of blue prints of Key Plans of the Building, — from Cellar to Attic, inclusive, — So that he may study them as he desires to do, to locate the library in it.

Aug. 12.
Pictures to Senator Merrill.

Carried over to Senator Merrill's committee

A page from Mr. Green's journal, containing the end of his entry for July 24, 1893, at the top. This page is from the notebook stamped "3" in red ink on the title page on which he inscribed a title, his name and position, and the indication that the journal was continued "from 2d Book" LC–USP6–6451–A

If the subject dealt with engineering, he spoke in flat statements and tones of pride as he cited mathematical accuracies—one senses the energies of a man in love with his work. If an interview involved the Library of Congress building, he spoke from a full knowledge of its every detail, and he explained in full. Since all its aspects interested him, he extended his knowledge—and therefore his discussions—to libraries, architecture, and library architecture in general.

Like many an interviewee, he apparently assumed at times that reporters had as much background on his subject as he. Small wonder that those reporters who were unfamiliar with the building's architectural origins gave him at times more than his share of credit in print. He spoke so knowledgeably about the building's architecture!

He was not afraid to take responsibility. When press criticism rose in 1895 over some of the sculpture and the subjects which Ainsworth Rand Spofford (Librarian of Congress from 1864 to 1897) had chosen for it with approval of "the architects in charge," Mr. Green was queried and replied bluntly:

> It was done by this office. There was no committee to consult. The whole of these details constitute a part of the decorative finish of the building, and in such matters it would take forever to refer everything to a committee. We just take the bull by the horns and go ahead. Of course, we have good advisors at every turn.
>
> We expect to get some criticism and some censure. In so great a work that is inevitable. . . . There may be other ways. We hope, however, that our way may always prove a good one. With that we shall be content. There may be others just as good; sometimes better.[17]

The personal clippings in the scrapbooks and his obituaries elsewhere depict a man who took part in community activities. He was an active member of All Souls' Church, which he served as a trustee and as Sunday school superintendent, and a member of the American Unitarian Association and of the Unitarian Club. He belonged to the National Society of Fine Arts and was a trustee of the Corcoran Gallery of Art and of the Union Trust Company. He joined the American

Association for the Advancement of Science and the National Geographic Society. He served as a director of the American Society of Civil Engineers, as treasurer of the Philosophical Society and of the Washington Academy of Sciences, as president of the Cosmos Club, and as an officer in other organizations.[18, 19]

While at the Library, he served as consulting engineer for the Corcoran Gallery, the D.C. Public Library, and the Pennsylvania State capitol at Harrisburg, as well as on private structures. He gave his advice informally on many projects, both public and private.[20] The Washington *Evening Star* reported that he served as "chairman of the President's consultative board on the location and design of public buildings." [19] A graduate of the Lawrence Scientific School at Harvard (B.S. degree, 1863), he was a participant in the Harvard Club's activities in Washington.

He retained his New England family ties. On New Year's Day in 1887 he was in his native Malden, Massachusetts, to attend the golden wedding anniversary of a relative, and there are many clippings about other members of the family.[21] He wrote a column about a trip to Mexico for the *Malden Mirror* of May 21, 1892.

And he was an ardent canoeist. When the Potomac Canoe Club to which he belonged and the Washington Canoe Club joined forces in 1888, the merger took place at his home.[22] A news item about the Potomac group in 1886 noted:

> Mr. Bernard R. Green has just purchased a fine canoe from Cumberland, and is an enthusiast on the subject of canoeing. He can view the Washington Monument from every objective point while seated in his little craft and take notes on its declination as seen from the river.[23]

He joined in meetings of the Washington Monument Society, which met at members' homes—among them that of Dr. Joseph Meredith Toner, the Library's first major donor. With Colonel Casey, Mr. Green once escorted a First Lady—Mrs. Cleveland—on a tour to the top of the monument.[24] He never lost interest in the structure's engineering. The day after the 1886 earthquake that wrecked Charleston, South Carolina, and sent tremors through Washington, a reporter putting down phrases that bear the brand of Bernard Green wrote:

> Mr. Green, Col. Casey's assistant, in charge of the Washington monument, made scientific observations of the structure. . . . The observation proves that the shaking had not the slightest effect upon the monument. In fact, the usual tendency of the structure toward the centre of the earth seems to have been arrested or rather reversed since the last observation, as the position as compared with that of one month ago is one-two thousandth part of a foot higher.[25]

The apparent contradiction of the last two sentences seems not to have struck the reporter or the editor in the outpouring of a much longer statement. In direct quotations, too, Mr. Green frequently went on from an opening flat statement to speak of all the possibilities of his subject. He was not an inarticulate man. Although his journal entries are brief and pointed, his statements to the press are lengthy—and the press did not stint him on space for his interviews. This is the man of whom the *Washington Post* wrote lyrically on July 11, 1897:

> All of his friends and many who know him only by reputation are glad that Mr. Bernard R. Green has been named as Superintendent of the new Library building. It is a case of the right man in the right place. No one could surely fill the position . . . so intelligently and acceptably as the man who has had charge of its construction from the very foundation. But Mr. Green has more than expert knowledge. He has an agreeable personality and knows just how to treat the public. . . . Mr. Green sees whoever asks for him, treats them in the pleasantest and most urbane way, never seeming to feel put out or annoyed by the countless demands made upon his time and patience.

In the Congressional debate about Mr. Green's promotion in 1896, Senator William B. Allison of Iowa called him "modest and unassuming" and "a man of high personal integrity of character." In the *Troy* (New York) *Daily Times* of April 16, 1892, a correspondent described him thus: "Industrious, energetic, honest to the last degree, a fine judge of men, and an expert of the very first rank" whose "great modesty goes far to hide his light under a bushel." Calling him "a doer rather than a talker," the writer admitted that he did not know where to find "a more interesting and instructive talker."

He had his share of press criticism, of course, during the contention over credit for architects John Smithmeyer and Paul Pelz versus the two engineers and the young architect who was General Casey's son. Nor did the press spare him in the spring of 1899 when the Women's Christian Temperance Union launched an attack on him for the alleged sale of "intoxicating liquors" (apparently wine and small beer) in the Library's cafeteria. This he flatly denied. When affidavits were produced from patrons, he denied the accusation that he had condoned it. The issue in the ensuing battle became so clouded in the news reports, with their delightful headlines, that the facts are hard to discern; but the ladies' attack was concerted enough that poor Mr. Green finally retreated from further public comment.[26]

One thing is notable. Whether the articles favored or embarrassed Mr. Green, they were clipped and saved. And the articles that favored Mr. Smithmeyer and Mr. Pelz or praised the latter's talents are pasted carefully into the record.

The journal depicts a diarist of sparse words and a stern disciplinarian on the job—a man impatient of human failings that slowed construction but a man touched by human sorrows. The scrapbook portrays a talkative man of social grace and broad interests, capable of long monologs and fascinated by the mathematical and engineering details of his own specialty.

Both point to a professional proud and sure of his work, even passionate about it. Together they indicate that his modesty was personal, his pride professional. He became loquacious when he was asked about the work itself—and was carried away on his own flood of information.

This was a man who could scold an artist for tardiness in fulfilling his commission [27] but comfort another with careful handling of his artistic work.[28]

The Double Harness

In an article about the Library building on October 4, 1891, the *Boston Sunday Globe* described Mr. Green as "a trusted friend of Gen. Casey" and the general's "executive man." The executive man's journal entries confirm that he returned the general's trust and friendship with almost reverent regard. The double harness fitted them well.

Their joint efforts on the Library of Congress project did nothing to diminish their repute. The work which had stalled in 1887–88 moved continuously forward in the eight years after the new brigadier general took over its completed excavation and half-finished foundation. When Mr. Green reported in 1897 that construction costs totaled $155,414.66 less than the $6,500,000 limit which Congress had set for that purpose, the luster of the reputations of the superintendent of construction and of the late General Casey could only be enhanced.

General Casey was at the Library building for planning and decisions—to consult with artists working on commissions, resolve problems with contractors, meet with Members of Congress and other officials concerned with the building, and appear before Congressional committees. He had his hand on many projects, however—including the District's suburban highways in the 1890's. Retired by the Army on May 10, 1895, he was continued in his post at the Library by Congressional action.[29] Five days before his death, the Washington *Evening Star* (March 20, 1896) found him "intensely concerned in this great project," keeping an eye on work progress personally and attending to details "with all the enthusiasm and keenness of interest" he had devoted to earlier projects "of great magnitude intrusted to his care."

Both men conferred with Librarian Spofford from time to time, giving him blueprints to study, asking his wishes on arrangements for the reading room or the collections, seeking his views on a proposed tunnel to the Capitol.[30] Although the Librarian had no responsibility for the construction, he was consulted on at least the literary aspects of the artistic decorations and was acquainted with artists commissioned by General Casey.[31] If he did not hold the reins of the harness, he was an avid and impatient passenger on the long journey to a building for his Library. The *New York Times,* asking him "How long before it will be completed?" in an interview dispatched on August 26, 1893, won a strong reaction:

"Four years at least," was the curt reply, and Mr. Spofford turned on his heel and walked away as if the mere thought caused him anguish.

A contemporary impression of this trio was recorded in the light, almost teasing tones of *The Capital,* a Washington weekly magazine, on July 13, 1895, two months after General Casey's Army retirement:

In the abandoned-looking old mansion at the corner of the new Library Grounds is the office of Bernard R. Green and he is the Superintendent of Construction of the new Library; and while he sits there much of the time in his office on the lower floor, making contracts with everybody, specifying just what shall be done, attending, in short, to the thousand and one details required to construct the finest library building in the world, he hops out among the three hundred workmen now and then, once or twice a day, say, and they tell me that if anything is going wrong, this remarkable man can detect it in a minute. General Casey is the engineer in charge. But Bernard R. Green is the real boss of everything; and General Casey is mighty glad to have it that way. Now and then, two or three times a week, perhaps, Ainsworth R. Spofford drives up to the abandoned-looking old house at the corner of the grounds to see Mr. Green or somebody about some detail of the interior; and he always seems to be in such a hurry! And he whips up his old nag so hard and seems to wish that he might push on the reins; and yet they tell me that this fine old nag never becomes excited enough to break into a gentle trot even. My, but won't the Librarian be proud when he has moved into his new library! And there will be his tunnel underground to the Capitol, and all of his pages, and his library fiends [sic], and book cranks will be about him. Think of six million dollars put into this beautiful design! And it will be finer still if the new Congress votes to take the squares opposite and put up a temple for the Supreme Court and the art works that this poor old government happens to possess.

Nothing moved as quickly as Mr. Spofford would have liked!

Yet, despite Mr. Green's occasional mutterings to his journal about a late delivery or a day's delay on masonwork in freezing weather, the overall picture is one of steady progress from 1889 until the mechanized and ornately decorated building was furnished and ready eight years later. And the portrayal of Mr. Green attending to a horde of details and hopping about the construction site fits the image that emerges from his records.[32]

Well and Quickly Built

The size and complexity of the structure must have contorted the average man's mental picture of the work when it was only a construction site—with work on its interior advancing in some areas before the walls were completed elsewhere. To this day, the size—470 by 340 feet or 3.66 acres of building on a site of 10.97 acres from curb to curb—and the maze of corridors and architectural variety perplex the Library's daily visitors. A *Star* reporter who toured the site alone in 1893 was perhaps the first person to ask the question, now so familiar to the staff, with which he began his story about the building on April 29: " 'Will you please show me the way out of here.' " A man with a wheelbarrow, guiding him to an exit, told him that the 170 men working on the site that day led a lonely life—he himself normally encountered only one or two men a day and had not seen his brother in another section for two weeks!

But by October 1895, despite all problems and hazards, the building had advanced sufficiently to house the unclassified copyright

Thomas Lincoln Casey (1831–1896). The sketch, based on a photograph by Bell of Washington, is reproduced from Harper's Weekly 28:839 (1884). LC–USP6–6503–A

deposits that were moved to it from a crypt in the Capitol that month. The *American Architect and Building News* had already (March 23, 1895) called it "a fine building, well and quickly built." When the last of the original houses on the site was demolished in March 1896,[33] the two engineers could move their office into the building, where the artists and artisans already had quarters. In March 1897, it was opened to tourists and stood ready to receive the books that were cleaned and moved with other library materials between April and November.[34]

The imposing grandeur of the Italian Renaissance greeted the crowds who came to look and wonder. In the building's pristine years, New Hampshire's pale gray granite, forming the exterior walls and Corinthian pillars, gleamed almost white, and the gold dome above them literally glittered. The outer rooms and halls formed a vast three-story rectangle, its facades broken by the projection of six pavilions somewhat higher than the wings between them: one pavilion at each of the four corners, a slightly larger one at the center of the east facade, and the largest and main pavilion of four stories at the center of the west facade facing the Capitol. In the center of the rectangle was the great octagonal rotunda, connected by passageways to the central pavilions at the east and west and by bookstacks to the north and south wings. These connecting links leading from the rotunda formed a cross within the rectangle and created four open courtyards between the bookstacks and the wings. The building was said to have 2,000 windows, among them those in the stacks.

Spacious and colorful marble halls in the palatial design of the Italian Renaissance welcomed the tourists—first bewildering and then intriguing them with the intricate ornamentation and the profusion of symbolism in works of art. Exhibition cases did not arrive until after the collections were moved, but most of the Main Reading Room's furnishings—which survived with little change for the building's 75th anniversary—were in place for public service by autumn. Mr. Green would lament, however, that 100 chairs for the 199 desks for readers did not arrive until three weeks after the official opening ("at last," he noted, as he often did). Nonetheless, the gigantic room beneath the arching dome was called resplendent long before it was used. The two elegant reading rooms for the Senate and House, also on the main floor but in the southwest wing and pavilion, would be ready for the next session of Congress.

The bookstacks and shelves, designed by Mr. Green, won praise in the library world. The arrangement of the Main Reading Room, with its alcoves for reference books and its convenience to the stacks, was lauded in the daily press. Much admired by reporters, too, was the machinery—especially the "railroads" that carried books from the stacks to the reading room and from the octagon to the Capitol via the underground tunnel.

But it was the artistic decorations that caught the public eye, drew the crowds, and won both praise and reproach in the press.

Asked by the *New York Daily Tribune* about the materials used inside the granite Library, Mr. Spofford was said to have remarked that there was "more marble in it than in any building in America." [35] Certainly the quantity and the 15 varieties of marble in nearly as many colors are impressive.

The floors are marble—often marble mosaic. The interior pillars are marble, their capitals richly ornamented. The stairs are marble, and the railings of the two grand staircases of the Great Hall are marble, intricately carved. The vaulted ceilings of the arches in the adjacent halls are marble mosaic. The fireplaces of the House and Senate reading rooms are marble with richly colored mosaics above the mantels. The Main Reading Room is a mass of marble up to the dome.

Scores of murals decorate the lunettes, panels, and pavilion domes of the upper floors. Gilded rosettes ornament the panels of the series of small domes in the corridors on the main floor. Decorative designs are painted on the arches of the ground floor and in every ceiling or wall left empty elsewhere. High and low plaster reliefs fill every niche and corner. Sculpture in bronze abounds.

Still, when the "new Library of Congress," as the writers of the day consistently called it, was officially opened for use on November 1, 1897, some of the sculpture was missing. Mr. Green had done *his* part—the building was up, the plumbing was in, the steamheat was tested, the lights were burning, the new mechanical gadgets were working. But the bases for some of the bronze figures in the fountain at the west front steps were empty, and above the exterior staircase curving up to the main entrance, only two of the three sets of bronze doors were installed. Inside, two of the 16 bronze statues for the Main Reading Room had not come—the artist responsible for both had not even modeled the second one yet.

Main Corridor

This drawing of the bookstacks for the Library's new building is signed "Bernard R. Green, Superintendent &
Engineer," the designer. LC–USP6–6506–A

And not only was the sculpture for the great clock incomplete, but the heavy serpentine hands designed by its artist were hindering the clock from its work.

That the building should lack several of the long-commissioned works of art may not have troubled Mr. Spofford or the new Librarian of Congress, John Russell Young—they had other concerns that day.

But sometimes it frustrated Mr. Green.

Authors of the Interior Designs

Seventy-five years later, a nine-year-old girl stared up at the ceilings above the Great Hall and turned to the Library's tour guide. "How did they paint it?—how did they get up there?"

A woman among the tourists who were clustered around the guide said that she was learning to make mosaics; she wanted to know how those in the vaults were done. One-third of the questions about the Library from that group in 1972 centered on the building itself.

A man asked: "Who chose the symbolism in the decorations?"

The answer to that question is not crystal clear, nor is it brief. Many hands were involved.

Paul J. Pelz, promoted to architect for the building by General Casey in October 1888 and retained through March 1892, wrote in 1895 that he had designed all parts of the building's exterior and had prepared preliminary sketches and drawings for all of the

Two reading rooms were designed in the new Library building for the use of Members of Congress. This unfinished room on the main floor of the southwest wing became the House of Representatives Reading Room. Beyond it in the southwest pavilion was the Senate Reading Room. Today, when Members of Congress make far greater use of the Library but find less time for personal research, the latter room serves as the Congressional Reading Room, and the room shown above houses the main offices of the Congressional Research Service.

Over the fireplaces at the north and south walls of this gallery are marble mosaics of "History" and "Law" by Frederick Dielman, a painter born in Germany in 1847 but brought in childhood to the United States, where he established a studio in New York in 1876 after his studies at the Royal Academy in Munich. LC–USP6–6533–A.

decorative work of the entire building. He added that the marble work of the corridors, Great Hall, and octagon were from his designs but that his successor—General Casey's son— had disregarded those sketches in redesigning the stucco work of the dome.[36] At the time, Mr. Pelz had not seen the work in other areas.

On August 11, 1891, Mr. Green noted in his journal a telephone call from a Dr. Magruder "Reporting Mr. Pelz illness" and its nature "to explain his absence since early in July." When Mr. Pelz returned to duty is not certain. The next entry to speak of him—unusually long for Mr. Green's jottings—is dated November 5, 1891:

Asked Mr. Pelz again what his plans were for completing designs and getting through here. Had a similar consultation with him last spring at which time it appeared and was understood that he would be through by Nov. 1, inst. or possibly January 1st next. He seems to think he should remain on indefinitely, but his work is nearly done, (should have been finished long ago) and he now understands that he must finish as soon as possible, say in two or three months, and cease connection with the office.

It was the task of one man to create new images in his mind and to translate them onto paper in lines, which are abstractions that do not exist in nature. The job of the other was to read them and to rear a building on the empty land—to put brick and stone and iron together in a tangible realization of the complex vision. That the goals were mutual and the roles complementary did not promise cooperation between the specific personalities. In retrospect, conflict between the disciplinary nature of the forthright engineer and the artistic sensitivities of the apparently retiring architect seems inevitable.

On February 1, 1892, Mr. Green wrote: "Arranged with Mr. Pelz, architect, that his *regular* employment on the Building should terminate on April 1, next."

Mr. Pelz, in the account cited earlier,[36] said:

Although it is the custom the world over to retain the architect, at least in a consulting capacity, until his building is finished, I was informed in the spring of 1892 that my services were no longer required, the reason given being "that I had completed the work that I was expected to do." General Casey's letter to that effect is highly complimentary and does not leave the slighest doubt as to my efficiency and attention to duties. My removal from the building was absolute and complete, as I have never since that time been called in consultation.

The architect's statement closed with the plea that, although he wanted his successor to have credit for his departures from the original designs "if his own work be meritorious above mine," he did not want to be held responsible for changes if they failed to harmonize "with what was put up from my design—prepared even before he had established himself in business. . . ." He disapproved of "radical" changes in the dome.

Edward Pearce Casey was barely 28 when he replaced the 50-year-old architect. He had been graduated from Columbia University's School of Mines with a degree in civil engineering in 1886 and received the Bachelor of Philosophy degree in 1888, the year his father took charge of the Library project. He spent the next three years in Paris, studying architecture at the Ecole des Beaux Arts, and returned in 1891 to open an office in New York City, where he made his headquarters until shortly before his death in 1940. He supervised the interior work of the Library of Congress building—literally cutting his professional teeth on it—and was adviser on its artistic decoration from December 1892 until 1897. His later career was not unsuccessful. He won a number of architectural competitions, and his colleagues in the American Institute of Architects raised him to institute fellowship in 1926. With Columbia's Prof. William H. Burr, he won first prize for a design for a new memorial bridge across the Potomac in 1900, and he designed the Memorial Continental Hall for the Daughters of the American Revolution (1904–7).[37]

He was generally credited at the time with the designs for the Library's interior. Critic William Anderson Coffin, a landscape and figure painter of the period, wrote in the March 1897 *Century Magazine,* for example, that "the amount of work done by Mr. Casey in designing the principal interiors of the building is enormous." And Herbert Small, who compiled several editions of a guidebook about the building at the turn of the century, told the touring public that Mr. Casey's designs "principally include all of the most important interior architecture and enrichment in relief and color." [38] This author cites Mr. Casey, too, as supervisor and adviser "in all matters of art." Under his direction were three artists who supervised all noncommissioned artistic work for the interior.

Exterior Sculpture

Certainly it was not young Casey who conceived the exterior's most remarkable sculptural feature: the keystone heads. He was still a student in Paris in January 1891, when their modeling began, and Mr. Pelz was still the building's architect.

Ornamenting each keystone above 33 appropriate windows on the building's main floor (the second story), where the traditional gargoyle might be expected, is a granite head about 18 inches in height. The features of each are sufficiently individualized to represent ethnological strains of the human race, based on data of that day, without attempting personal portraiture.

William Boyd, who modeled many of the sculptural features of the granite exterior, and Henry Jackson Ellicott, a local sculptor who had studied at the National Academy of Design and under Brumidi,[39] modeled the heads in collaboration with Prof. Otis T. Mason, curator of the Department of Ethnology at the Smithsonian Institution, on the basis of photographs, measurements, and life-size models then in the collections there.

Mr. Green's first mention of any of this trio is dated December 11, 1890, in the earlier notebook. A John G. Craig visited him that day "—By request to talk stone carving." He was

Edward Pearce Casey (1864–1940). Taken during his service with the 7th Regiment of the New York National Guard, this photograph is reproduced from The Casey Family of East Greenwich, *a lecture delivered by the Reverend Charles Albert Meader and reprinted from the East Greenwich* News *of September 5, 1927.* LC–USP6–6501–C

followed by "Mr. Ellicott, modeller for Sup'g Architect—Ditto." The next references are dated March 23, 1891, when he reported the "carving and modelling shed about finished and work begun in it," and March 30; both references appear in the notebook begun that month. In the first entry he noted:

Visit from sculptor Ellicott again at my request, and arranged with him to make a keystone head model on trial.

On March 30 he wrote:

Visited Mr. Ellicott's modeling studio at 19th & H Sts. N.W. this morning with Mr. Boyd and Prof. Mason, to see Ellicott's first model of one of the 1st story keystone heads, the Australian. Thence Prof. Mason and Ellicott came up to see Mr. Boyd's first head,—the Japanese.[40]

The next October, in the article cited earlier from the *Boston Sunday Globe,* Mr. Green was asked "Where did you get those heads?"

"It became necessary," said the engineer, "to put something upon the keystone of windows as large as those, and it has been the habit in the past to carve fantastic heads such as the people in the middle ages were thinking about with their mixture of piety and diabolism.

"It occurred to me that over in the National Museum were models taken from the life of nearly all the races— at least all the American races, and I suggested to the custodian in ethnology there, that we use these heads upon the public library.[41] He warmly entered into the idea, for he is strong in that hobby."

Conventional keystones appear on the Smithmeyer & Pelz design which won an architectural competition held by Congress in 1873 and on their September 1888 version. But among the varied plans they produced for Congress in the intervening years is an 1885 design whose keystones bear faces. And when Congress told General Casey to produce a $4-million plan, Paul Pelz sketched faces on

This representation of the Chinese people is among the 18-inch ethnological heads sculpted in granite on the 33 keystones over the main floor windows of the Library's 1897 building. The photograph is by Willy Arnheim, a stone construction inspector of Albany, N.Y.

three keystones in his November 1888 drawings. In neither case are the sketches so detailed as to indicate ethnological features. No faces appear on Mr. Pelz' $6-million plan, which won final approval in 1889, but several appeared on the building by August of 1891.

No other news reports credit Mr. Green with the idea—indeed, like Herbert Small later in his books, they are silent about its origin. Certainly Mr. Green took pride in the keystone heads—the Chicago *Sunday Herald* of November 13, 1892, noted that Professor Mason was "no prouder of them" than Mr. Green; but it gives the latter no credit. Mr. Pelz claimed all the exterior design.

Did Mr. Green suggest Professor Mason's collection as models for Mr. Pelz' idea? Was the reporter taking shorthand notes? Or did he jot down the main points and later—in a very long article with nine paragraphs in direct quotation—attribute all to the man who poured out a stream of data? In any case, a lie by Mr. Green to take credit for another man's work appears out of character.

Mr. Pelz' 1888–89 drawings certainly depict a fountain between the lower exterior steps at the west front of the site. His 1888 drawing for the design adopted by Congress features statuary on the exterior, too—although not in its present forms or locations. Mr. Boyd's four colossal figures of Atlas, supporting the pediments of the west main pavilion, and the nine portrait busts on the main portico, high above the third-story level, apparently supplanted Mr. Pelz' earlier designs.[42]

Each of the nine three-foot portraits in granite at the top of the portico walls is pedestaled before one of the nine circular windows which throw the sculpture into relief —and which Mr. Green aptly called "the bullseye windows." The men portrayed are, from north to south, Demosthenes, Emerson, Irving, Goethe, Franklin (centered to give him preeminence), Macaulay, Hawthorne, Scott, and Dante. The busts of Demosthenes, Scott, and Dante were modeled by Herbert Adams,

18

sculptor of the eight pairs of Minervas (Peace and War) in the west foyer leading into the Great Hall, of one of the Main Reading Room's bronzes, and of Washington's McMillan fountain. The busts of Emerson, Irving, and Hawthrone are by J. Scott Hartley, a sculptor from Albany, New York, who had exhibited his work in London. Those of Franklin, Goethe, and Macaulay are the work of F. Wellington Ruckstuhl, winner of a grand medal at the 1893 Chicago Exposition and sculptor of the Main Reading Room's bronze Solon, "Evening" in the Metropolitan Museum of Art, and works in other cities. The portico's sculpture was completed mainly in 1894. Mr. Green received the last three pieces on January 31, 1895, and had them mounted in late March.

Far below the portrait busts is "Neptune's Court," the stone fountain with its mythological bronze figures at the extreme west front of the Library's site. Fitted snugly into the retaining wall of the small hill that rises from the west sidewalk, it is centered between two staircases leading to the main plaza of red Missouri granite and to the exterior grand staircase of the main floor entrance. Visitors who approach the building via the semicircle formed by the driveway and its walks often miss this appealing feature.

Roland Hinton Perry completed the bronze sculpture in the fountain when he was 27. (The dolphins in relief on the stone wall above the figures were modeled by Albert Weinert, however.) A New Yorker who studied at the Ecole des Beaux Arts in Paris in 1890 and at two other academies in that city in 1890–94, Mr. Perry was a portrait painter as well as a sculptor. In addition to the figures for Neptune's Court, he created the four sibyls in bas relief in the vaults at the ends of the north and south corridors on the Library's west main floor. His plastic works also include numerous memorials in various cities.[39]

The fountain's bronzes arrived piece by

piece over 11 months. Mr. Green had the stone bases ready on the day after Christmas, 1896. On February 26, 1897, he wrote: "Putting the two *Tritons* of the fountain in place. Mr. Perry here superintending." The following October 6 he added: "One of the nymph groups of the bronze fountain arrived at the Building from Henry-Bonnard Bronze Co., the other group to complete the fountain is still due." The

Between the Corinthian pillars at the center of the west main pavilion's portico is this three-foot bust of Ben Franklin, by Frederick Wellington Ruckstuhl. The circular window behind each of the portico's nine portrait busts was intended to throw each bust of granite into greater relief than the granite walls could provide. The ornamental sculpture of the façade was designed by Albert Weinert. LC–USP6–6542–M

"other group" did not arrive in time for the Library's official opening—the next journal entry about the sculpture is dated January 26, 1898:

—The 3rd and last group (north) of the fountain bronzes arrived yesterday. Hoisted into fountain basin today to be put together and set up.

It was February 23, nearly a year from the first delivery, before he could finally write: "Bronze fountain finished by the setting of the last (northerly) group and trimming the stone work." [43] Nevertheless, Mr. Green expressed neither impatience nor disappointment over its belated completion. Mr. Perry had taken on the massive job when another artist did not fulfill the original assignment.

Mr. Green expressed no impatience in his journal over the late delivery of the missing bronze doors for the west main entrance, either. There was sad reason for their delay.

Facing west toward the U.S. Capitol is the Library's "Court of Neptune" fountain on First Street, Southeast. The pool of its stone basin is 50 feet long. The colossal Neptune in the center would be 12 feet tall if the figure were standing. Before each grotto at either side of the sea god is a Nereid riding a sea horse, and two Tritons flanking Neptune stand in the pool blowing water from conchs. Jets of water crisscross the pool from a sea serpent, two frogs, and four turtles.

Five of the building's nine granite portico busts may be seen on the portico of the west main pavilion: Emerson, Irving, Goethe, Franklin, and Macauley. Beyond Macauley, but out of view in this photograph, are Hawthorne and Scott. Demosthenes is on the north side of the portico and Dante on the south side. LC–USP6–5030–C

Olin Levi Warner, born in Connecticut in 1844 and some months younger than Mr. Green, had studied sculpture in Paris before setting up his studio in New York. He had already sculpted one set of the double bronze doors and had begun another when he died in August 1896. He had completed another work for the Library of Congress—the marble re-

From the second floor of the Great Hall, this flight of steps leads to a pair of staircases which flank the landing and which lead in turn to the Visitors' Gallery overlooking the Main Reading Room. The marble mosaic seen above the staircase landing in this early view represents "The Minerva of Peace." A curious feature of the colorful mosaic is that from either the right, center, or left staircase, Minerva's toes appear to point toward the viewer. Elihu Vedder, a New Yorker working in Rome, completed this work when he was nearing 60 and also painted five murals entitled "Government" in the tympanums adjacent to the entrance to the Main Reading Room on the lower floor. Photograph from the Monographs of American Architecture *(Boston, Ticknor, 1898).* LC–USZ62– 47261

liefs of "The Students" on the spandrels of the Great Hall's central arch, opening toward the Main Reading Room. They appear immediately below this commemorative arch's frieze, where "Library of Congress" is inscribed in large gold letters.[44]

Herbert Adams completed the set Mr. Warner had begun, and these doors arrived the same day as the last sculpture for the fountain, January 25, 1898. The work of setting them in position began the next day and was finished on February 19.

The three sets of massive bronze doors—14 feet high, 7½ feet wide from frame to frame, and weighing some 3½ tons together—are set in the three arches of the grand entrance to the main floor and its Great Hall. In the granite spandrels above them are six life-size figures representing, from north to south, "Literature" (composition and writing), "Science" (pure and practical), and "Art" (sculpture and painting). These are the work of Bela Lyon Pratt, also a native of Connecticut who had studied in Paris. About 30 years old when the building was opened, he was the sculptor of the bas-reliefs of "The Seasons" in the four pavilions on the second floor (third story)[42] and of one of the symbolic plaster statues in the Main Reading Room.

The doors Mr. Warner completed are in the northernmost arch of the main entrance—at the left as one faces the building. The tympanum above them represents "Tradition" and depicts a woman telling past lore to a boy. The figures on the doors symbolize "Imagination" and "Memory."

The tympanum above the central doors, the work of Frederick Macmonnies, shows the Minerva of learning and wisdom diffusing the products of typographical art, and the figures in the doors symbolize "The Humanities" and "Intellect." Mr. Macmonnies, a native of Brooklyn who studied in New York and Munich as well as Paris, sculpted one of the bronzes in the Main Reading Room, and his "Pan of Rohallion" came to the northwest courtyard in the 1930's as the gift of Mrs. Gertrude Clarke Whittall.

Above the southern doors by Mr. Warner and Mr. Adams is a tympanum symbolizing "Writing." The figures on the doors themselves represent "Research" and "Truth." [45]

The Golden Quilt

Who decided to gild the dome above the octagon is not clear, but gilded it was. Mr. Green was very proud of it. According to one news report, he waved a thin gold leaf in the air while explaining its properties to the re-porter. He recorded the gilding process almost step by step.

"Began gilding the finial for the dome lantern," he noted on August 14, 1893, while he was checking the stonework's steady progress in the northeast pavilion and the installation of window lintels in the second story. A week later: "Put up the gilded finial tip (flame) on the dome and removed scaffold of same." And on August 31: "Fairly began gilding of dome lantern—4 gilders being at work on it." The lantern was finished by September 9.

Problems had arisen meanwhile—the main copper ribs of the dome were found to hold

Bela Pratt's life-size granite figures were completed in the spandrels above the three archways at the main entrance above the outer staircase of the west main pavilion when this 1895 photograph was made. The bronze doors had not yet been completed, and the set for the doorway at the right—interrupted by the death of sculptor Olin Warner—was not installed until 1898. Among the Corinthian pillars on the portico above, the third column from the right is the replacement for the shaft that crashed and splintered on July 24, 1893. LC–USP6–6527–A

water in the scale ornaments and had to be "altered somewhat, causing delay." "—Copper finish on dome still unfinished," he worried on September 14. "Gilding of main dome awaiting it." Meanwhile, the top story stones of the west main pavilion were being set, interior marbles were going into position in its Great Hall, and contracts were being let for pipe-covering while window jambs were installed. Mr. Green interrupted his own work to see to the hoisting of 13 bells to the top of the building, where they would remain long enough to be rung for the centennial of the laying of the cornerstone at the Capitol.

On Friday, October 13, a heavy southeast gale came up, complete with rain. At 4:30 P.M., the gilders' protective awning was blown from the dome. The men worked late "to prevent great damage to both copper work and gilding which they accomplished."

But by November 14, nearly three weeks before he carried General Casey's annual report across the street to the Capitol, he could say: "Finished the dome gilding. Quantity of gold leaf used was $3391\frac{12}{20}$ packs of which about 42 packs were used on the lantern crown and finial." Herbert Small reported the total cost, including the gilding for the flame on the "Torch of Learning" that surmounts the dome, to be "less than $3,800."

Vaulting high and free above the forbidding fence that kept intruders away from the construction below, the golden dome must have blazed over Capitol Hill. There were hints in the press that it competed with the Capitol dome.

The Cincinnati *Enquirer* was one of the first to call attention to the appearance of the two domes on Capitol Hill, although fairly objectively. In a dispatch published on November 5, 1893—headed "A House of Great Beauty" and subheaded "How It Compares with the White-Domed Capitol"—the writer pointed out: "The Library dome is gold, while the Capitol dome is iron, painted white." He called the building "the third conspicuous

object in the city" (after the Capitol and the Washington monument). The *Washington Post* said early the next year:

The gilded dome may not win the unfeigned admiration of every beholder and is already the subject of some critical remark, but it is not well to pass hasty judgment on this crowning feature of the building. We can judge better of its general effect when the building is finally completed. . . . The impression of the critics . . . is that a more subdued tint would be preferable and in better keeping with the distinctive characteristics of the great edifice. . . .

The Washington *Evening Star* of February 17 called it "a golden quilt" in a story billed as "A CHAT WITH MR. SPOFFORD." The Librarian is not quoted, but among other information is a great deal of data about various gold domes and their cost. The reporter states that the gold on the dome at Washington did not cost one-tenth the amount of the dome of St. Isaac's in St. Peterburg. On June 1, 1894, the *Star* added: "The new Congressional Library building . . . does not, of course, pretend to rival in size or grandeur of outline the splendid classical edifice at either end of which the houses of Congress sit, and in the center of which the Supreme Court holds its sessions." The *Post* even called the dome "strikingly beautiful" the next September 17.

None of this local defense stopped the fine arts critic for the *Independent* of New York, Sophia Antoinette Walker, from stating flatly on April 23, 1896:

As the train rolls into Washington the old primacy of the Capitol dome is disputed by a gilded dome rising from a vast white granite building. So near is the new architectural feature that perspective lends undue prominence, and one is disturbed that the classic dignity of that most beautiful of civic buildings, the Capitol, should be lessened by its neighborhood. But it is from one side only that the dome, which is comparatively low and flat, rising upon an octagonal base at the intersection of the central pavilions of the Library, can make this unfortunately aggressive appearance; and one soon congratulates himself if a minor dome was to be (and what violations of good taste have not been perpetrated in the public buildings?) that it emphasizes the importance of the building which holds the heritage of the ages. . . .

The gold leaf proved to be the least of the dome's problems, however. Mr. Green's worries with water in the scale ornaments the year before were only the beginning. As early as 1912, rain and snow were infiltrating the dome, and there are constant reports of repairs in the years up to 1931. Finally a section of the copper covering was removed and held up to the light, which revealed hundreds of tiny perforations, hardly large enough for a needle to penetrate. The fault was laid to the fact that the copper had been tinned, a practice no longer followed by the time of the investigation into the leaks, and it was speculated that free acid between the copper and the tin coating was eating into the metal.[46]

The Librarian's annual report for fiscal 1932 (p. 299) noted only that the copper covering of the dome and lantern had been replaced. On October 30, 1931, however, in a report headed "Library Loses Gold Dome for One of Copper," the Washington *Herald* explained:

Copper sheeting is being used to replace the gold leaf, which has gradually been losing its glitter for many years. . . . The copper, in time, will glisten in the sun just as does the statue of the goddess on the Capitol dome. . . .

Asked whether the new copper would be gilded as the 1897 copper had been, William C. Bond, superintendent of the building, told the reporter that this would not be decided for two or more years. The news report continues:

It has been thought that the Library, colored by the wear and tear of the elements, would not harmonize well with a new gold dome.

The effect of time on the copper roofing will be noted before any final decision is made, however.

Mr. Green's golden quilt had disappeared. In time, the new copper would wear a patina of pale green.

Three years later, the Washington *Evening Star* reported on December 18 that, although there had been no White House announcement, "it is known" that the Chief Executive had asked the Architect of the Capitol, David Lynn, to consider refacing the Library building and removing its dome.

The latter, the President thinks, is "out of tune" with the Capitol dome and, therefore, should be eliminated. His attitude is supported by professional critics who for years have insisted that the modified Italian Renaissance style of the Library contradicts the Classic style of other monumental structures in Washington. The carved exterior decorations, these objectors have argued, are "gingerbread."

The next morning, the *New York Times* reported that President Roosevelt, in reply to queries, had said that "he did not contemplate spending Federal money merely to beautify or alter existing buildings for esthetic reasons for some years to come while there was a pressing need for additional working space."

There were those who deplored the proposal. Edward Alden Jewell wrote in his column in the arts section of the *Times* (January 13, 1935) : "I am not convinced that such unity would be a good move." Nearly 35 years later, the Library's Main Building was listed in *The National Register of Historic Places, 1969,* prepared by the Office of Archeology and Preservation, National Park Service.[47]

The Interior Decorations

Like a number of the commissioned artists, the three supervisors who were in charge of the building's decorations under Mr. Casey were contemporaries of the young architect.

Elmer Ellsworth Garnsey, an artist two years his senior, supervised the general color decorations. He had studied under George W. Maynard and Francis Lathrop in New York, where he had been a student at the Cooper Institute and the Art Students' League. Credited with work at the World's Fair, he also decorated the Boston Public Library and the Carnegie Library in Pittsburgh.[39] The elaborate arabesques in the halls and the color schemes in all the rooms in the Library of Congress building are attributed to him. Artists William A. Mackay and Frederick C. Martin worked on

24

Artists and artisans created the Main Building's decorations in impromptu studios inside the walls long before construction ended. A shed was built in the northwest corner of the grounds for the marble carvers in December 1892, but they were moved inside on December 8, 1893, to make their quarters in the northwest wing on the main floor. This picture of October 16, 1894, however, shows them at work in the northeast wing. The windows at the left were blocked off in the late 1920's by the addition of a new bookstack in the courtyard, and two windows in the right foreground were blocked with the addition of the Rare Book Room in the early 1930's.

The large eagle at the right of center and one of the two matching eagles at the left (shadows make exact identification difficult) flank the marble tablet above the Great Hall's commemorative arch; all three eagles are the design of Albert Weinert. Philip Martiny's cherubs for the railings of the grand staircases in the Great Hall can be seen in the foreground, and Corinthian capitals are everywhere. The men who roughed out **the designs by compressed-air cutter before the finer work began were called "Air Chisel Artisans" in a** Washington Post *head-line of December 21, 1894. LC–USP6–6524–A*

the finer portions of the wall designs. W. Mills Thompson and Charles Caffin made the final cartoons from the original sketches for the frescoes. Some 25 fresco-painters were employed for about 18 months under artist Edward J. Holslag as foreman.[38]

Heading the modelers for the stucco ornamentation of the halls and galleries was Albert Weinert, creator of the dolphins above "Neptune's Court." Born in Leipzig, Weinert had studied at the school of fine arts in Brussels before immigrating to the United States. His work was represented in the Panama-Pacific Exposition in San Francisco, and he created monuments and memorials in a number of cities—among them Lord Baltimore's statue in the city named for him.[38, 39] He was about 31 when Mr. Green recorded his arrival at the Library on April 19, 1894:

Albert Weinert, sculptor, came yesterday to arrange for engagement as chief modeller for the dome and other vault surfaces. Engaged him @ $10. per day.

The following Monday, Mr. Green added:

Weinert, modeller, began laying out his work and getting ready to begin modelling for the dome. Shop being fitted up in N. C. 2nd story.[48]

The last member of the supervising trio was from Milwaukee and the same age as Mr. Weinert. Herman T. Schladermundt was in charge of the Library's abundant mosaics and the stained glass for the skylights and the rotunda's windows. Mr. Casey prepared the preliminary sketches for the vaults and some of the stained glass and Mr. Schladermundt the final cartoons. The latter's work was in the Columbian Exposition at Chicago in 1893, and he painted murals for the grand jury room in Newark, the Flagler Memorial Church in St. Augustine, and the Emigrants' Industrial Bank and the Museum of Thomas F. Ryan in New York.

Beyond this trio of young men and their even younger director were the commissioned artists, more than fifty American sculptors and painters, as Mr. Small and the critics were

proud to underscore. The Government, said Mr. Small, "had never before called upon a representative number of American painters and sculptors to help decorate, broadly and thoroughly, one of its great public monuments." *Leslie's Weekly* on October 11, 1894, called for thanks "for what the functionaries at Washington have given us, for be it said that these works on and within the Congressional Library will start American sculpture upon a new plane, and mark a new era in plastic art in the western hemisphere."

The Main Reading Room Sculpture

On that happy note, *Leslie's Weekly* concluded a column that wondered mildly about the men chosen to be represented in the nine portico busts and in the 16 bronze portrait statues for the Main Reading Room. The *Boston Evening Transcript* had already raised one or two questions on August 15, 1894, but said of the announcement of the 25 "immortals" that "Mr. Spofford, Librarian of Congress, has made a comprehensive selection of the greatest writers of all time. In most respects it seems to be a wise judgment. . . ."

Kate Field's Washington, however, published with approbation on October 3 a long letter from Sarah Freeman Clarke of Marietta, Georgia, protesting the exclusion of women from the list of "immortals." Pointing out that "a considerable portion of the readable books in this library are written by women," she made a case for including Harriet Beecher Stowe in the list. The die, however, if not the statuary, was already cast.

No primary source stating that Mr. Spofford made the selections has been located—only the clipping above and other news reports of the time, including the one in which Mr. Green proclaimed that "this office" did it.

The *Philadelphia Press* of November 6, 1894, noted that General Casey had been in consultation for a year with the National Sculptors' Society and had issued commissions in cooperation with J. Q. A. Ward, Augustus St. Gaudens, and Olin L. Warner in planning the statuary. Mr. Green confirms this in a journal entry of January 26, 1894, stating that these three sculptors "came on request at 10:30 A.M. Met here by the General and myself who accompanied them through the Building. Object: Discussion of sculpture required in Building. The visitors left about 2 o'clk, agreeing to consider and report as to work and cost."

All commissions for the 25 "immortals" and all but one for the eight symbolic plaster statues in the reading room had been issued when the *Boston Evening Transcript* reported the announcement in August.[49] Although the portico works were in place by the next spring, the last of the bronzes did not arrive until the end of 1898.

The eight plaster statues, symbolizing features of civilized life and thought, are above the eight marble columns of the octagon and below the springline of the dome. Each is 10½ feet tall. The literary or biblical passages inscribed in gold on the tables above them were selected by Harvard's President Eliot.[38] On the gallery railing below them are the 16 bronze portrait statues of men prominent in the fields represented by the plaster statues. The 24 statues, clockwise from the Visitors' Gallery are:

Science, by John Donoghue

   Newton, by Cyrus Edwin Dallin
   Joseph Henry, by Herbert Adams

Law, by Paul Wayland Bartlett
   Kent, by George Edwin Bissell
   Solon, by Frederick Wellington Ruckstuhl

Poetry, by John Quincy Adams Ward

   Shakespeare, by Frederick Macmonnies
   Homer, by Louis St. Gaudens

Philosophy, by Bela Lyon Pratt

   Plato, by John J. Boyle
   Bacon, by John J. Boyle

Art, by François Michel Louis Tonetti-Dozzi, after sketches by Augustus St. Gaudens

   Michelangelo, by Paul Wayland Bartlett
   Beethoven, by Theodore Bauer

History, by Daniel Chester French

   Herodotus, by Daniel Chester French
   Gibbon, by Charles Henry Niehaus

Commerce, by John F. Flanagan

   Columbus, by Paul Wayland Bartlett
   Fulton, by Edward Clark Potter

Religion, by Theodore Bauer

   St. Paul, by John Donoghue
   Moses, by Charles Henry Niehaus

Mr. French's "History" was the first model to arrive—May 18, 1895. It was cast on the floor of the rotunda beginning May 23, and the sculptor finished it June 5, Mr. Green noted. From then on, notes about the arrivals of the statues are scattered throughout the journal entries into 1896 and 1897. Among them are intermittent reports about the great clock for the reading room and its massive bronze sculpture of "Father Time," for which John Flanagan in Paris was commissioned.

But when the reading room was opened for service on November 1, 1897, Columbus and Michelangelo were still missing. Mr. Green must have been under a great deal of pressure that autumn, overseeing the eternal moving of the books, making trial runs of the book carriers, hastening the last contractors. Only twice does his journal reflect real impatience with an artist, and of those occasions, apparently the artist knew it only once. Paul Bartlett, a 32-year-old sculptor and painter from Connecticut, who studied under Rodin and who sculpted the equestrian statue of Lafayette in the Louvre, got the full brunt of Mr. Green's frustrations on November 20, 1897:

Bronze statue of *Columbus* arrived at last from Henry-Bonnard Bronze Co. N.Y., and so did the sculptor Paul W. Bartlett from Paris. I took him to task for his delay in fulfilling his contract of 3½ years ago and the fact that the third piece,—statue of

Sculptor John F. Flanagan may have been five years late with his bronze of "Father Time," but his plaster statue of "Commerce" rose from the rubble of construction in the rotunda months before the Main Reading Room was opened for service. On February 15, 1896, Bernard R. Green noted in his journal that the artist's "figure of Commerce, arrived here in pieces (2 boxes) from Paris and was put up in the Reading Room today." A native of Newark, N.J., Mr. Flanagan studied at the Ecole des Beaux Arts in Paris, where he won several medals and prizes, and was about 30 when he produced this figure. His works are held by art museums in Paris, Ghent, New York, Chicago, and Pittsburgh, and he created a bronze of Samuel Pierpont Langley for the Smithsonian Institution, as well as a tinted marble relief of Aphrodite for New York's Knickerbocker Hotel. LC–USP6–6532–A

Michael Angelo,—is not yet modeled. This, he said he could not stand and precipitately left the room and finally left the building without returning to the office.

Mr. Green had Columbus placed on his pedestal the very next day—a Sunday!

Michelangelo did not arrive until December 22, 1898. He was hoisted upon Christmas Day.

But the clock was Mr. Green's longest trial. He had years to wait yet.

The Interior Dome

Mr. Weinert's stucco ornamentation of the dome's interior has 320 square blue panels, bordered in gold and ivory and containing gold rosettes. Among them is a bewildering variety of putti, eagles, lions' heads, sea horses, dolphins, griffins, and other figures in relief. The overall effect is impressive, if overwhelming, and lends a pale richness to the warm tones of brown and redbrown in the room below, where Tennessee, Siena, and Numidian marbles rise in tiers toward the dome. In the collar of the dome and in the ceiling of the lantern above it are two murals.

On September 20, 1895, one week after Walter Acton fell to his death in the rotunda, Edwin H. Blashfield arrived from New York with an assistant to mount the scaffolds to the highest points. A New Yorker of 47, who had studied under Leon Bonnat at Paris in 1867 and at London's Royal Academy for several years, Mr. Blashfield had shown his work at the Paris Salon in 1874–79, 1881, and 1891–92. In the collar of the Library's dome, he painted a mural of the stages in man's intellectual development, completing it on March 7, 1896. Later, in the lantern he depicted "Human Understanding" as a woman lifting her veil to look beyond finite knowledge; a cherub on one side holds a book, and another looks down toward the figures in the collar below with a gesture of encouragement.[38]

The figures in the collar—each about 10 feet tall—had human counterparts, if not models in all cases. Although Mr. Blashfield did not

The heart of the Library's reference service to the public is its Main Reading Room, and the great octagon in the rotunda beneath the dome is architecturally the central feature of the Main Building. Behind the bronze statues on the railing of the upper gallery are the partitions which were erected in the 1960's to provide work space and which were removed in the summer of 1980. LC–USP6–6175–C

The dome's collar painting is Edwin Blashfield's concept of the evolution of western civilization. The dome springs from the entablature above the upper arches in the line of an exact half-circle and is 100 feet in diameter at the springline. Between the eight ribs, gilded and set in cream-colored moldings, are 320 coffers with gold rosettes; the coffers diminish from 4½-foot squares of deep blue at the springline to 2½-foot squares of light blue at the collar. LC–USP6–6543–M

attempt portraiture in this instance, some of the figures are recognizable.[38] Twelve in number, they begin at the east side of the collar, apparently in salute to the East as the cradle of civilization, and represent contributions to western civlization.

"Egypt" is depicted by a man with a tablet of hieroglyphics bearing the seal of Mena and a group of papyrus books, denoting written records. "Judea," representing religion, is a woman praying near a stone pillar inscribed "Thou shalt love thy neighbor as thyself." "Greece," for philosophy, is a crowned woman holding a scroll by a bronze lamp.

"Rome," for administration, is a man in a centurion's armor and lion's skin. "Islam," for its introduction of physics, mathematics, and astronomy into Europe, is an Arab with a book of calculations.

Actress Mary Anderson was the model for the "Middle Ages," the period in which modern languages emerged in Europe; she holds the sword and cuirass of chivalry and leans on a cathedral representing Gothic architecture. Amy Rose, a New York sculptor, inspired the figure for "Italy," representing the fine arts and holding a palette and brush; near her are a violin, a replica of Michelangelo's David, and the capital of a Renaissance column.

Notations in Mr. Green's journal indicate that Mr. Blashfield did not complete all the drawings for his conception of the collar before beginning to paint. The entry for October 1, 1895, states: "Mr. E. H. Blashfield nearly completed the first 2 figures in the dome crown ("Modern Languages") and returned today to N. York for a few weeks to work up more material." He came back to paint the north and northeast portions, then departed for New York again on December 14, leaving his assistant to "go on with the work" during a 10-day absence. On February 27, 1896, before the collar was completed, he "tried his full size cartoon in place for the lantern area, dome." With him were General Casey and Mr. Green. Ten days later he finished the collar painting. In it was General Casey, from whom "Germany" was modeled. The general, representing printing, turns from a handpress to examine a proofsheet.[38]

A New York painter, William Bailey Faxon, was the model for a 16th-century Spanish adventurer holding the tiller of a ship. "England," for her contribution of literature, has the face of actress Ellen Terry, who is crowned with laurel and holds a book of Shakespeare's plays, opened to *A Midsummer Night's Dream.*

"France," representing emancipation, bears the features of Mrs. Blashfield; the figure is seated on a cannon, carrying a drum, bugle, and sword, and displays a scroll with "Les Droits de l'Homme" inscribed upon it. "America," symbolizing science, is represented by an engineer holding a scientific book and leaning his chin on his hand near an electric dynamo. His features recall those of Abraham Lincoln.

From this scaffold designed by Bernard R. Green, the interior of the Library's dome was decorated in 1894–96. The illustration is from the Scientific American *LXXV:364 (November 14, 1896). LC–USP6–6529–A*

Mr. Flanagan's Clock—At Last

The artist's rough plaster sketch for the clock had arrived from Paris on July 1, 1895, and a larger model on April 7, 1896. The marble work for the clock was installed on February 12, 1897, and two boxes of clockworks were delivered by the E. Howard Company on March 18 and installed a month later. There were problems, however, and the workmen

were back several times. On November 26, 1897, Mr. Green noted that they took away the clock's hands "to be made straight instead of serpentine as modelled by the artist."

The dial of the clock is four feet in diameter, with a gilt sunburst in its center. It is surmounted by a life-size bronze figure in high relief of Father Time, who is flanked by maidens and children representing the seasons. A student sits reading a book on either side of the dial, which is set against a mosaic background containing the signs of the zodiac in bronze.[38]

But in 1897 there was only the clock. On November 25, 1898, the bronze bas-relief, "Swift Runners," to be set in the marble below the clock, arrived. Finally, on June 23, 1902, the signs of the zodiac came from Paris, followed by the "long expected group of 'Time'" on June 30 and the artist. Up went a scaffold and up went 1,600 pounds of bronze. It took two days—Saturday and Sunday, July 26 and 27—before the sculpture was bolted into place. In his second irritation with an artist—and in one of the rare entries of personalized remarks about another man—Mr. Green vented his feelings on his journal: "Flanagan present and nosing about, talking irrelevantly, asking questions and giving useless directions as usual."

Two weeks later (Saturday, August 9), he recorded this:

—After much "fussing" over the details of the clock sculpture, its setting and coloring, also efforts of Flanagan to apply a new pair of serpent hands the latter were temporarily attached today and the whole work considered completed. A photograph is to be made by sculptor (Flanagan) tomorrow. The new hands are too heavy for the works of the clock and not of satisfactory shape and form. The old plain hands will therefore be restored and Flanagan proposes to supply a new light pair in the future. Whether he does or not the present old pair will answer.

Mr. Green did not put much stock in those artistic hands. Nevertheless, the hands on the clock today are serpentine.

The next entry is dated August 19, 1902:

—John Flanagan, sculptor of R. Rm. clock, finally said good bye today and said he was going to New York, intending to look for work and to establish a studio in that city.

It is the last entry. For Bernard Green, the long construction job was done. The building he loved was completed—insofar as that was possible—and for the next decade, except for one lesser construction project, he would simply keep it running, which is not an easy task. But the "Journal of Construction" was ended, and he added no postscripts.

The Twentieth Century

By its nature, the building can never be complete.

First, it houses a library, born to grow in any era. More, it is the home of the national library, and the Nation stood in 1897 on the threshold of an age of explosions in knowledge, in populations seeking after knowledge, and in technological communication of knowledge. The Nation's monument to the printed record of civilization had to grow with the Nation.

"The Librarian of Congress a century hence will not find himself cramped in the least," boasted the Washington *Evening Star* on July 14, 1894, in a happy account of the building's spacious accommodations for the future growth of the collections. It was an innocent assurance in an innocent age—who could foresee the 20th century?

But as early as fiscal 1907, Bernard Green reported to Congress[50] on the unanticipated "geometrical progression" in the growth of the collections, which had already "generally occupied" the 10-year-old building. He proposed construction of a new bookstack in the southeast courtyard; by 1910 it was in use. By 1930, the northeast courtyard was filled with another bookstack, and an addition to the east front provided for a Rare Book Room in 1934.

Meanwhile, a gift from Mrs. Elizabeth Sprague Coolidge had made possible the construction of an auditorium for chamber music in the northwest courtyard in 1925; the courtyard was enhanced in 1928 by her gift of a small reflecting pool. In 1939 a pavilion given by Mrs. Gertrude Clarke Whittall to house her gift of Stradivari instruments was opened in the same courtyard.

By 1939, when he opened the Library's new Annex Building for public service, Librarian Herbert Putnam (1899–1939) had relived Mr.

Spofford's long struggle to acquire space for the crowded collections and for staff to serve them. Not even half the projected century of spaciousness had passed.

More and bigger explosions of knowledge and printing were yet to come. The collections of about a million books, manuscripts, maps, music, and pictorial items that had come from the Capitol in 1897 had multiplied 25 times by the end of World War II. In the next quarter century, despite selective acquisition, they more than doubled again, and demands for service to meet the new needs of Congress, other libraries, and scholars became imperative.

During the 1960's, cellar space, storage space, and exhibition halls were turned into workspace. Partitions went up in marbled pavilions and corridors. By 1964, staff began to be moved to rental quarters, and, ultimately, even some of the collections had to be housed in other buildings. Soon the Library's operations were scattered over an area stretching 65 miles across Virginia, Maryland, and the District of Columbia, with staff members providing national library services in cramped or alien quarters. Like Mr. Spofford and Mr. Putnam, Librarian L. Quincy Mumford (1954-1974) had come to know the painful need for space.

But in 1971, ground was broken for the Library of Congress James Madison Memorial Building. With its dedication on April 24, 1980, Librarian Daniel J. Boorstin gave new names to the older buildings: the Library of Congress Thomas Jefferson Building (1897)

In the Great Hall, the staircase hall beyond the foyer of the main entrance stretches 72 feet from the six stained glass skylights topping the west main pavilion to the floor three stories below. The signs of the zodiac, interspersed with rosettes, are depicted in the brass inlays on the floor. The central inlay is a sun with the four points of the compass pointing to the building's main axes.

The sculpture of the two grand staircases of white Italian marble is the work of Philip Martiny, an Alsatian who came to the United States in his early twenties and who studied in Paris under Eugene Dock and in this country under Augustus St. Gaudens.

On each newel post is a bronze figure of a woman wearing classic drapery and a laurel wreath; both hold electric torches aloft and are 6½ feet tall (8 feet to the tops of the torches). In the staircase railing Mr. Martiny symbolized the fine arts, the four continents, and 16 occupations with 26 putti, which the marble cutters called "the babies" and which they carved first with air chisels, then with handtools.

On the lower railing of the north staircase are a gardener with rake and spade, an entomologist with a butterfly net, a student with his book, and a printer with his types, press, and typecase. On the upper railing are a musician with his lyre and music, a physician grinding drugs, an electrician with a telephone receiver, and an astronomer with a telescope measuring a globe with his compass.

On the lower railing of the south staircase are a mechanic with cogwheel and pincers to symbolize invention, a hunter with a gun and a dead rabbit, an infant Bacchanalian with a glass of champagne, and a farmer with his sickle and sheaf of wheat. The upper railing features a fisherman with his catch, a soldier polishing his helmet, a chemist with a blowpipe, and a chef with his cooking pot.

The railing of the second landing on each staircase contains the cherubs representing the four continents— Asia and Europe at the north, America and Africa at the south. The putti on the railing of the upper landing at the north represent painting, architecture, and sculpture. Those at the south symbolize comedy, poetry, and tragedy.

In each of the four corners of the coved ceiling at the top level, Mr. Martiny modeled two female half-figures of stucco supporting a cartouche which bears a lamp and book to symbolize learning. Above them are figures of flying genii painted by Frederick C. Martin. In the 10 penetrations containing the windows that open onto the fourth level of the main pavilion are tablets inscribed with the names Dante, Homer, Milton, Bacon, Aristotle, Goethe, Shakespeare, Molière, Moses, and Herodotus.

The main floor's east gallery, glimpsed through the lower arches, and its north and south galleries have vaulted ceilings of marble mosaic. Full-size cartoons for these mosaics were drawn by Herman T. Schladermundt after sketches by Edward Pearce Casey, then transferred to thick paper and coated with thin glue, on which workmen placed the stones smooth-side down. The ceilings were coated with cement, the stones applied, the paper soaked off, the design pounded in, and the stones pointed off and oiled but not polished.

and the Library of Congress John Adams Building (1939). Books and staff began to be moved to new quarters. By summer, the ugly partitions in the Visitors' Gallery of the Main Reading Room and in the 1897 exhibition halls had come down, as promised long ago, to reveal magnificent galleries that many Americans had never seen before.

The 19th-century palace has survived such plastic surgery with a modicum of grace. She has aged, and the galleries now restored to their original purposes need to be restored to their original beauty. But her intrinsic character can be clearly seen and still astonishes the eye.

Like all much-used public buildings, the 1897 monument requires the constant care of Mr. Green's successors. The Architect of the Capitol now assigns about 135 people to the maintenance of the three Library buildings.

On the Library's own staff are more than 165 special police and a housekeeping force of about 165 people. A building whose exhibit halls are open to tourists 13 hours daily and 10½ hours on Sunday—every day but Christmas—requires staffing in two shifts every day for some jobs. Special police and maintenance personnel are on duty in three shifts through 24 hours a day and handle any problems that develop when the building is closed. The doors are locked at 9:30 P.M., but the Library is never deserted.

Special jobs and contract work are required beyond the normal maintenance. In 1958, for example, the Great Hall's decorative skylight, chipped and even broken in places by weather, had to be repaired. A successor to the company of Heinigke and Smith, installers of the original stained glass, proved to have in its storage bins quantities of the same glass used in that skylight—more than 60 years later. In 1962, the building's granite face, blackened with the soot and grime of years, was steam cleaned for the first time. The stone emerged in excellent condition, the beauty of its architectural details sharply delineated for the first time in many years.

The Main Reading Room—where service had never been suspended for more than a day or two for special occasions—was completely closed for one year, three months, and 12 days in 1964–65 for the first phase of the work to install a new heating and ventilating system for the entire building. While the room was closed, workmen cleaned and renovated it, installed new lighting, and restored the works of art.

Again, a great scaffolding rose to the dome in fascinating geometric patterns—a photographer's field day and a challenge to a few staff members who dared climb the bright red metal bars to sense the room's size from dizzying heights.[51] A second scaffold was built in the lantern for the cleaners and painters, and a huge parachute was opened upside down beneath the lantern to catch the splatters.

The blackened portrait statues and Mr. Flanagan's sculpture were restored to their original bronze color, the stucco and plaster works were cleaned and painted, the marble was washed and polished. When the room was opened again in the late summer of 1965, it could be seen in its original splendor for the first time in more than a generation—but more clearly than ever, for the new lights illuminated both readers' desks and works of art as never before.

Mr. Green would have been proud.

NOTES

[1] The quotation is from the entry for July 24, 1893, p. 70–71, of the "Journal of Operations on the Building for Library of Congress. Continued from 2nd Book, Mar. 16, 1981, and concluded. Bernard R. Green, Sup't and Engineer." Manuscript Division.

The entry contains no mention, however, of the weather conditions or of the stage of construction, information derived from newspaper reports.

[2] *Ibid.* The measurements of the shaft and its tonnage were obtained from Gerald T. Garvey, chief of the Library's Buildings Management Office.

[3] *Ibid.* Two discrepancies occur between Mr. Green's account and that of the *Washington Post* of July 25, 1893: "William H. Cochran, a white man, thirty-seven years of age, living in Alexandria, and employed on the

Congressional Library, had his left forearm badly mashed by a falling stone about noon yesterday." The news report adds that the victim's arm had been amputated at Emergency Hospital by a Dr. Karr. Mr. Green's entry may have been based on excited reports from the scene of the accident, or the reporter may have obtained secondhand information by telephone.

[4] *Ibid.,* entry for Jan. 26, 1894. In December 1896, an article about Mr. Green's scaffold was headlined by the *New York World* as "THE GREATEST SCAFFOLD IN THE WORLD." The writer stated that it was designed with such mathematical accuracy that it was used in its rotary action "to verify the structural exactness of the dome at every point," a phrasing reminiscent of Mr. Green's manner of speaking on many engineering subjects. The upper traveling scaffold cascaded like a stairway in a series of platforms from the top of the dome toward its base, resting on a small trolley circling the base of the dome and rotating on an axle set in the lantern above the dome and supported by the massive beams of the main scaffold rising from the floor of the rotunda. In the lower traveling scaffold, another series of platforms was suspended vertically from the base of the dome for work on the areas below.

[5] *Ibid.,* entry for Sept. 13, 1895; and the *Washington Post,* Sept. 14, 1895, p. 2. The *Post's* account of the accident itself coincides substantially with Mr. Green's journal except for the *Post's* report that the victim fell 80 feet "to the ground" and that the accident occurred "in the main entrance hall" (which is 72 feet in height.) Mr. Green reported that Walter Acton was "employed as a water boy by Snead & Co. Iron Works on the furring and lathing of Main Stair Hall vaulting," but that he "fell through the scuttle in the *rotunda* scaffold nearly 70′ clear to *1st* floor. . . ." (Italics added).

[6] Record book of the Commission for the Construction of the Congressional Library Building (untitled, except for the words "Record" and "Library Building Commission" stamped on the spine), in which the entries date from Apr. 16, 1886, through June 14, 1888. Library of Congress Archives, Manuscript Division. The minutes indicate Apr. 1 as the effective date of the appointment; apparently no one noted at the time that it fell on Sunday. The Washington *Sunday Herald* of that date reported that Mr. Green moved his office effects on Saturday to the Commission's office at 145 East Capitol St. and would take charge on Apr. 2.

[7] Joint Resolution No. 35, 54th Congress, 1st Session, passed by the Senate on Thursday, Mar. 26, and by the House on Monday, Mar. 30; approved by the President on Thursday, Apr. 2, 1896.

Questions were raised briefly in both houses about the haste. The *Congressional Record* for Mar. 26 has Senator William E. Chandler of New Hampshire explaining: "The reason for the haste is, that although there are contracts made, and numerous contracts, there are a great number of people who are working upon the Library building day by day and people who are receiving compensation by the day, and large compensation is being paid for the decoration and ornamentation of the building. They have no authority to continue their work for a day or an hour unless we shall by some method devolve the control of the building upon some one."

In the House on Mar. 30, Representative Lemuel E. Quigg of New York noted the approaching end of the month and the fact that "it will be very unfortunate for a great many people whose compensation depends on the signature of the superintendent of construction unless we pass the resolution before the first of the month." Representative Leonidas F. Livingston of Georgia was moved to ask whether General Casey had yet been buried (he had—on Mar. 27) and was told that Mr. Quigg did not know but that "the great Government of the United States must go on." Both Mr. Allison and Mr. Livingston raised the possibility of letting the duties devolve upon General Casey's successor in the Corps of Engineers, but Mr. Green's knowledge of the project—and Congressional knowledge of him—won the day.

[8] Washington *Evening Star,* June 30, 1897.

[9] *Report of the Librarian of Congress and Report of the Superintendent of the Library Building and Grounds for the Fiscal Year Ending June 30, 1914* (Washington, 1914), insert facing p. 6. According to the Librarian's *Report* for fiscal 1922 (p. 7–11), the post of superintendent was abolished by an act of June 29, 1922, transferring its structural and mechanical responsibilities to the Architect of the Capitol and its custodial and housekeeping duties to the Library.

[10] Mr. Green's first six months, while John L. Smithmeyer was still architect for the construction and Paul J. Pelz assistant architect, must have been an interesting period, for the engineer was responsible directly to the Commission and his salary at that time exceeded that of Mr. Pelz. Hired at $4,000 a year, Mr. Green had felt the duties—"the most arduous, exacting, and responsible of any under the Commission"—to be worth $6,000, or at least $5,000 (the salary of Mr. Smithmeyer), but was apparently convinced by the members that the feeling in Congress would sustain no more than they offered him. (When Mr. Pelz was later promoted to architect by General Casey, his salary was raised to $4,000.) If Mr. Green kept his journal in those first six months, however, that portion has not been located with the other two parts retained in his office.

One of the two extant notebooks bears no title and contains entries dating from Oct. 4, 1888, through

Sept. 29, 1893; it deals chiefly (but not exclusively) with visitors, jobseekers, Congressional relations, and similar matters.

The other notebook bears his handprinted title and bold signature on the flyleaf: "Journal of Operations on the Building for the Library of Congress. Continued from 2d Book, Mar. 16, 1891, and concluded. Bernard R. Green, Sup't and Engineer." The entries from Mar. 16, 1891, through Aug. 19, 1902, deal mainly with construction (notably its progress in each aspect, although not on a daily basis), contracts and contractors, events affecting construction and materials, the work of the artists, and related matters.

The phrase "continued from 2d Book" and the overlapping dates of the two notebooks with their differing natures indicates that the titled notebook may have been continued from an earlier notebook, possibly one that covered construction from Apr. 1, 1888, to Mar. 16, 1891.

[11] Washington *Evening Star,* Mar. 26, 1896 (obituary of General Casey).

[12] *Ibid.* The construction of one wing and most of a second wing for the State, War, and Navy building between 1871 and 1877 had cost more than $6 million. Colonel Casey and Mr. Green completed the second wing and built the two remaining wings and central section in time for occupation on Mar. 1, 1888, for less than $4 million. Yet Librarian of Congress Ainsworth Rand Spofford, in an apparent reference to the cost-cutting for the Library's building, said of the Army's Chief of Engineers in the *Star*'s obituary of the latter: He was "economical without being parsimonious."

The work of excavating beneath the partial shaft of the Washington Monument and replacing its foundation with a larger base of concrete ran from Jan. 28, 1879, to May 28, 1880; after four years more to finish the shaft, the capstone was set in December 1884, and the monument was dedicated the next Feb. 22.

[13] Record book (see note 6).

[14] W. M.—Mr. Green's customary abbreviation for West Main, referring to the main pavilion at the center of the building's west front.

[15] The scrapbook, in three volumes marked "A," "B," and "C," contains entries from February 1885 through March 1911 and was the gift of Dr. Julia Minerva Green and her brothers—Bernard Lincoln, William Ezra, and Arthur Brooks Green—in October 1950. Manuscript Division.

The clippings bear primarily the expected titles of Washington newspapers and national magazines but range among a number of out-of-town newspapers as well. They fall into five categories.

The majority deal with construction projects on which Mr. Green worked; most numerous among them are those about the Library of Congress. A smaller group deals with architecture and engineering in general. In another are frequent stories about friends, colleagues, and their relatives—and often their obituaries. The smallest category involves the personal activities of Bernard Green and his family.

Nearly as large as the first group is a miscellany of widely varied nature. There are a number of religious articles and others about churches, art objects, music, and scientific phenomena. The obituary of Sitting Bull, an article about the Rosetta Stone, and an 1892 interview with the last man to have seen Lafayette buried are among the wide-ranging subjects of others. More intriguing are the frequent verses scattered throughout the volumes, chiefly from newspapers and often doggerel; lists of noms de plume of current authors; and groups of autographed pictures of literary lions and a generous number of lionesses from issues of *Harper's New Monthly Magazine.*

The latter, together with a discourse on the "virtues of a true woman of the world," inspire wonder about the keeper of the scrapbook. Was Mrs. Green—or daughter Julia, who became a physician—the wielder of the scissors and paste pot?

The presence of so many personal clippings—and the fact that the scrapbook was not retained in Mr. Green's Library office but was a later gift from the family—would indicate that it was maintained at home. The stamp of his engineering and architectural interests is so heavy in it, however, that the work as a whole has a masculine flavor. Then, too, the clippings on religious, scientific, and artistic subjects are supported by his membership in organizations devoted to science and art and by his extensive church activities. His interest in the articles on music is reflected in the fact that he served on the music committee of his church, belonged to the Choral Society of Washington, and sent one son (William) to Europe to study the violin.

Presumably, he at least approved the scrapbook's contents. There is some evidence that he kept the record himself, however. The clippings continue chronologically, for example, throughout a long period when Mrs. Green was reported by the *Washington Post* (July 11, 1897) to have been in Boston on an extended visit to their daughter, who was attending medical school there.

The last clippings are from the spring of 1911, three years before Mr. Green's death, when the Washington *Evening Star* (Oct. 22, 1914) reported that he had been in failing health for some years. Mrs. Green and their children survived him. Each volume bears his name, printed in ink but in an unidentified hand—possibly that of a member of the family.

[16] Washington *Times,* Dec. 6, 1896.

[17] *Ibid.,* Sept. 9, 1895. The quotation appears at the end of the article in response to a discussion by the

reporter of the 25 men selected for portrayal in the portico busts and reading room statues. The article's main burden, however, is its first half, which inspired its heading, "Cherubs Minus Clothes," by lashing out at Augustus St. Gaudens for nude putti on the building's exterior—sculpture for which Albert Weinert was assigned responsibility. The writer was not sure whose work they were but was certain that "if he [St. Gaudens] is not responsible for the cherubs . . . the work will at least remind a great many people of him." The artist is scolded for importing customs from Paris, "where he got his training. . . ."

[18] *Washington Post*, Oct. 23, 1914.

[19] Washington *Evening Star*, Dec. 28, 1907 (Mr. Green's 64th birthday), and Oct. 22, 1914 (the day of his death).

[20] *Report* (see note 9).

[21] *Malden Mirror*, Jan. 8, 1887.

[22] Washington *Sunday Herald*, May 20, 1888.

[23] *The Capital* (Washington), June 13, 1886.

[24] *Washington Post*, Jan. 22, 1887.

[25] *National Republican*, Sept. 2, 1886.

[26] Various articles in several Washington newspapers in March 1899.

[27] Green, "Journal of Operations," entry for Nov. 20, 1897.

[28] Regina Soria, *Elihu Vedder: American Visionary Artist in Rome (1886–1923)* (Rutherford, Fairleigh Dickinson University Press, 1970), p. 219–20.

[29] Public Law 53–189.

[30] From entries in the "Journal of Operations" and the scrapbook. Among Mr. Green's clippings are many about Mr. Spofford—both interviews concerning the Library and more personal articles, including a report from the *Boston Herald* of Aug. 31, 1893, about a family reunion of 300 Spoffords, and the obituary of the Librarian's wife, Sarah Partridge Spofford, from the Washington *Evening Star* of May 11, 1892.

[31] Soria, *Elihu Vedder*. During this artist's 1895 visit to Washington in connection with his commission, Mr. Spofford entertained him at dinner, an occasion Mr. Vedder recalled later with delight, although he must have lacked the marvelous memory on which he complimented his host, for he apparently recorded the Librarian's name as Richard Spofford. Other artists were about the building as it was being occupied and during the next five years, until the last—John Flanagan—departed in 1902.

[32] Mr. Green must have been somewhat embarrassed, however, by the reference to the "real boss." His early journal entries note problems the general handled—for example, Mr. Green took a contractor, who claimed he had lost money on the work, to General Casey for interpretation of the contract and solution. By the time the general retired from the Army in 1895, however, the magazine writer's description may have been fairly close to the fact. The remarks of the *Star* reporter about General Casey's activities in March 1896—if read in their entirety in the article cited earlier—have a tone of condescending amazement that the man should be so active. General Casey was not quite 65 at the time; he was dead the next week, however. The age (or youth) of the reporter is not known.

[33] Washington *Evening Star*, Mar. 20, 1896.

[34] David C. Mearns, *The Story Up to Now* (Washington, Library of Congress, 1947), p. 138–40: "Chutes, Whip Tackle, Handbarrows, and the Crossing."

[35] Feb. 2, 1896.

[36] *American Architect and Building News*, June 29, 1895, p. 134.

[37] Henry F. Withey and Elsie Rathbone Withey, *Biographical Dictionary of American Architects (Deceased)* (Los Angeles, 1956); *and Who's Who in America*, vol. 17 (Chicago, 1932). Mr. Casey and Prof. Burr also won the competition for Washington's Connecticut Avenue bridge. The architect of a number of churches and memorials, Mr. Casey won first prize for his Grant monument in 1902 and for the Second Reform Church in Hackensack, N.J.

It may be noted that Mr. Pelz was barely 32 years old when he set to work on the first designs for the Library of Congress building—those that won the competition. He had begun his apprenticeship at the age of 18 under Detlef Lienau and had become a draftsman in Lienau's New York office in 1864–66 before launching his career as an architect in Washington. He was educated at the college of St. Elizabeth and the College of the Holy Spirit in Breslau, but at 16 he left before graduation to join his father in the United States, according to data in *Who Was Who in America, 1897–1942,* and the dictionary cited above.

[38] *Handbook of the New Library of Congress*, compiled by Herbert Small (Boston, 1901), p. 7–8. This work has been used for reference in several passages about the building's works of art.

[39] *Mantle Fielding's Dictionary of American Painters, Sculptors, and Engravers,* compiled and published by James F. Carr (New York, 1965).

[40] The ground floor of the Library's Main Building is called the basement, a proper term but one which many Americans now interpret to mean "cellar," and the main floor—the second story above ground—is called the first floor. Mr. Green refers here to the latter.

[41] The D. C. Public Library was not established until 1896, and because the Library of Congress was to be open to the public, many Washingtonians apparently thought of it as the local public library.

[42] The reference here to the "third-story level" of the main pavilion is in terms of the stories as seen by the stranger viewing the building's exterior.

The main pavilion, unlike the wings, has a fourth story above ground and beneath its attic. In the system of numbering described in note 40, this fourth story is properly called the "third floor." Adding to the confusion is a staff habit—handed down over the years—of calling this last level "the attic." The attic of this pavilion is actually above the fourth story but is closed off. When the last phase of the air conditioning for the main building was under way in the summer of 1969, the attic was opened for the installation of machinery, and this writer climbed the workmen's steps to view the interior. In the dim light could be seen a series of fascinating brick arches—fascinating because they repeat the style of the Italian Renaissance that dominates the building's "showcase" rooms.

[43] The basin of the fountain later developed leaks. See *Report of the Librarian of Congress and Report of the Superintendent of the Library Building and Grounds for the Fiscal Year Ending June 30, 1917* (Washington, 1917), p. 212.

[44] Above the Library's name is a marble tablet, forming part of the parapet of the balcony above the Great Hall and reading:

ERECTED UNDER THE ACTS OF CONGRESS OF
APRIL 15 1886 OCTOBER 2 1888 AND MARCH 2 1889 BY
BRIG. GEN. THOS. LINCOLN CASEY
CHIEF OF ENGINEERS U.S.A.
BERNARD R. GREEN SUPT. AND ENGINEER
JOHN L. SMITHMEYER ARCHITECT
PAUL J. PELZ ARCHITECT
EDWARD PEARCE CASEY ARCHITECT

[45] More detailed information on these doors and a description of the bronze doors of the Rare Book Room and the Annex Building are contained in a free, illustrated leaflet entitled *The Bronze Doors of the Library of Congress,* available upon request from the Central Services Division.

[46] *Hearings before the Subcommittee on Legislative Appropriations of the House Committee on Appropriations for Fiscal 1931,* 71st Congress, 2d Session (Washington, 1930) p. 185–87.

[47] Published by the Department of the Interior (Washington, 1969). Only Smithmeyer and Pelz are credited for the building. The entry errs in describing the style of the building as French Renaissance.

[48] N.C.—Mr. Green's abbreviation for "North Curtain," i.e., the north wing. In his day, the architectural term "curtain" was used, correctly, to describe the section of a building connecting two towers or other structures—in the case of the Library's building, the corner pavilion and the main pavilion. It is used frequently today, however, to refer to a nonbearing wall.

[49] "Religion" was the plaster statue for which a commission had not yet been awarded. It was created by Theodore Bauer, whose work was exhibited by the National Sculpture Society, but for whom biographical data is scarce and would be welcomed. The name "Dozzi," which appears on the statue of "Art" and which was recorded by Small in his early handbook only as "a French artist, M. Dozzi," has been identified as Tonetti-Dozzi by Isabelle K. Savell in her book THE TONETTI YEARS AT SNEDENS LANDING (New York, Historical Society of Rockland County, 1977). The artist later dropped the second half of his family name. Bissell is represented in the Metropolitan Museum of Art. Statues by Boyle and Dallin are in Chicago's Lincoln Park; Dallin won medals in U.S. and French expositions. Donoghue is known for his "Young Sophocles" and "Hunting Nymph." French sculpted the Lincoln Memorial's figure of the President and the "Minute Man of Concord." Niehaus did sculpture for the Senate Gallery and the Capitol's Statuary Hall, and Potter's equestrian statuary can be seen in Boston, Philadelphia, St. Louis, and Paris. Augustus St. Gaudens had a successful studio in New York, where his brother Louis also worked. Ward, the first president of the National Sculpture Society, did statues for parks in Washington and New York.

[50] *Report of the Librarian of Congress and Report of the Superintendent of the Library Building and Grounds for the Fiscal Year Ending June 30, 1907.* (Washington, 1907), p. 90–91.

[51] The view from the level above "History" was splendid.

The Main Building of the Library of Congress

A CHRONOLOGY, 1871-1980

by John Y. Cole

December 1, 1871. Librarian of Congress Ainsworth Rand Spofford suggests a separate building for the crowded Library, then housed in the Capitol.

1872. Spofford outlines the necessary features in the proposed structure, which must meet the needs of "a great national library."

March 3, 1873. Congress authorizes a competition to design plans for the new Library. A three-man commission is appointed "to select a plan and to supervise the location and erection of a building." A sum of $5,000 is appropriated.

August 1873. The competition is announced and a prospectus containing the specifications of the proposed building is issued.

December 22, 1873. The architectural firm of Smithmeyer & Pelz of Washington, D.C., is awarded the $1,500 first prize for its Italian Renaissance design. A total of 28 designs were entered in the competition by 27 different architects or architectural firms.

June 23, 1874. The competition is reopened when Congress appropriates $2,000 "to procure additional designs."

January 1, 1876. Librarian Spofford reports that he has run out of shelf space in the Library and that books, maps, and works of art are now "being piled upon the floor in all directions."

June 8, 1876. The Joint Library Committee, chaired by Senator Timothy O. Howe, recommends that the new Library building be located on the site of the Botanic Garden.

April 3, 1878. Congress appoints a six-man commission "to consider the whole subject of providing enlarged accommodations for the Library" and appropriates $2,500 for its use.

June 11, 1878. The commission reports that a majority of its members favor the construction of a separate building on Judiciary Square. The minority prefer a location across the east plaza from the Capitol.

December 5, 1878. President Rutherford B. Hayes urges a new Library building in his State of the Union speech.

March 31, 1879. Senator Justin S. Morrill supports a separate building east of the Capitol in his speech "The Library of Congress, the Capitol, and its Grounds."

May 5, 1880. Senator Daniel W. Voorhees exhorts Congress to action: "Let us . . . give this great national library our love and our care."

June 8, 1880. Congress establishes a Joint Select Committee on Additional Accommodations for the Library, chaired by Senator Voorhees, and appropriates $5,000 for its use. The committee appoints three architects, John L. Smithmeyer, Edward Clark, and Alexander Esty, to investigate the feasibility of enlarging the Capitol for the use of the Library.

September 25, 1880. The three consulting architects report against extending the Capitol and in favor of a separate Library building. As requested, each submits his own design.

February 10, 1881. Spofford reports to the American Library Association that architect Smithmeyer's Italian Renaissance design has been chosen by the Joint Select Committee.

December 6, 1881. President Chester A. Arthur asks Congress to take action on the Library building question.

March 13, 1882. Gen. Montgomery C. Meigs, engineer of the Capitol extension of 1853–59, states his opposition to a proposal to raise the dome of the Capitol 50 feet in order to provide additional space for the Library.

October 1882. Joint Select Committee sends Smithmeyer to Europe to examine other national library buildings.

December 8, 1885. President Grover Cleveland recommends a new Library building.

April 15, 1886. Congress authorizes the construction of a Library building according to the Italian Renaissance design of Smithmeyer & Pelz on a site adjacent to East Capitol Street. A building commission consisting of Secretary of the Interior L.Q.C. Lamar (chairman), Architect of the Capitol Edward Clark, and Librarian Spofford is placed in charge. A sum of $500,000 is appropriated to begin construction, and a limit of $550,000 is placed on the cost of the property.

May 17, 1886. The building commission recommends a location immediately south of East Capitol Street and between First and Second Streets for the Library.

July 31, 1886. District of Columbia Supreme Court authorizes the purchase of the houses and property of the site for $585,000.

August 5, 1886. Congress appropriates the additional $35,000 needed to obtain the property.

October 1, 1886. John L. Smithmeyer appointed architect.

October 28, 1886. Clearing of the site begins.

August 24, 1887. Work stops while cement for foundation is tested. The principal excavations are complete, and the drainage system has been laid.

January 17, 1888. William F. Vilas succeeds Lamar as Secretary of Interior and chairman of the building commission.

February 15, 1888. Cement controversy is resolved and work begins on laying the building's foundation.

February 16, 1888. House of Representatives appoints a Special Committee to Investigate Contracts for the Construction of the Library Building, chaired by Representative Thomas S. Holman.

March 19, 1888. Bernard R. Green appointed superintendent of construction.

June 19, 1888. House of Representatives votes to stop construction on the new Library building.

October 2, 1888. The Building Commission is dissolved and Congress places Gen. Thomas L. Casey of the U.S. Army Engineers in charge of construction. He is to be assisted by Bernard R. Green. A sum of $500,000 is appropriated to continue construction and Casey is instructed to submit a new plan for a building not to cost more than $4,000,000.

October 3, 1888. John L. Smithmeyer is dismissed and his former assistant, Paul J. Pelz, is appointed as the new architect.

November 23, 1888. General Casey submits his $4,000,000 plan but no action is taken.

December 1, 1888. General Casey submits two proposals for the consideration of Congress: his $4,000,000 design and the more elaborate $6,000,000 Smithmeyer & Pelz design.

March 2, 1889. Congress approves the $6,000,000 plan.

September 14, 1889. Concrete foundation for the building completed.

June 9, 1890. U.S. Court of Claims awards Smithmeyer & Pelz $48,000 for their design of the Library building.

August 28, 1890. Cornerstone for the Library is laid in the northeast corner.

December 1, 1890. General Casey reports that the cellar, the ground floor, and a considerable part of the first story have been finished.

October 15, 1891. The last of the 33 ethnological heads ornamenting the keystones of the first story pavilion windows is put into place.

December 3, 1891. General Casey reports that the first story has been completed and that the walls of the courtyard stacks and the Main Reading Room have reached the second story. The iron stacks have been installed.

May 1, 1892. Paul J. Pelz is dismissed as architect.

June 1, 1892. Beginning of a six-month strike of granite cutters in Concord, New Hampshire. Granite work on Library building delayed.

December 1892. Edward Pearce Casey appointed architect of Library building and placed in charge of interior design and decoration.

January 23, 1893. U.S. Supreme Court upholds earlier Court of Claims decision in *Smithmeyer & Pelz* v. *the United States.*

February 20, 1893. Joint Select Committee supports General Casey's use of foreign marble and brick in the construction of the building.

December 4, 1893. General Casey reports that the second story and the dome have now been completed. The dome, including the Torch of Learning at its apex, has been coated with 23-carat gold leaf.

January 26, 1894. Casey and Superintendent Green meet with sculptors J. Q. A. Ward, Augustus St. Gaudens, and O. L. Warner to plan the sculpture for the Library's interior.

June 1894. Announcement of the nine famous writers selected to be honored with granite busts across the west facade of the building and the sculptors of each. Herbert Adams will model Dante, Demosthenes, and Scott; J. Scott Hartley will furnish the busts of Emerson, Hawthorne, and Irving; and F. Wellington Ruckstuhl will prepare the likenesses of Franklin, Goethe, and Macaulay.

July 7, 1894. Last stone in the superstructure set in place.

August 1894. Announcements of the subjects for the eight symbolic statues for the inner dome and their sculptors, as well as the subjects for the 16 bronze portrait statues of illustrious men and their sculptors.

March 29, 1895. Green and Spofford agree on the interior arrangement of the Main Reading Room.

April 16, 1895. Placement of the nine granite busts across the west facade of the building completed.

April 1895. Announcement of painters to decorate building.

September 13, 1895. Workman killed when he falls 70 feet from scaffold.

March 25, 1896. Gen. Thomas L. Casey dies.

April 2, 1896. Bernard R. Green placed in charge of completing the building.

April 7, 1896. Edwin Blashfield completes his painting, "The Evolution of Civilization," in the collar and the lantern of the dome.

July 9, 1896. The names of the engineers and architects responsible for the Library building are inscribed in a commemorative arch on the east side of the staircase hall.

November 11, 1896. The decoration of the Librarian's office is completed.

November 16, 1896. Beginning of a special hearing by the Joint Library Committee to consider the organization and management of the new Library.

January 18, 1897. Librarian Spofford presents a statement describing the special rooms and facilities needed in the new building for the proper functioning of the Library.

February 5, 1897. Last of the paintings in the interior of the building is completed.

February 19, 1897. Library reorganized and its staff increased. Bernard R. Green placed in charge of the building and the surrounding grounds.

April 9, 1897. Transfer of materials to the new building begins with the removal of the books and pamphlets donated by Joseph M. Toner from the basement of the Capitol.

April 22, 1897. Superintendent Green reports that the net cost of the new building was $6,032,124.54, a sum $200,000 less than the total appropriation for construction.

May 28, 1897. Marble mosaic of Minerva, by Elihu Vedder, put in place on staircase landing leading to the Visitors' Gallery.

September 1, 1897. Library in the Capitol closes and full-scale transfer of materials to the new building begins.

November 1, 1897. New Library building is opened to the public.

November 20, 1897. Transfer of materials into the new building is completed.

November 25, 1897. Over 4,700 visitors take advantage of special Thanksgiving Day hours of opening to tour the new building.

February 19, 1898. The last of the three bronze doors at the main entrance is put into place.

February 23, 1898. The fountain in front of the building, designed by Hinton Perry, is completed.

July 8, 1898. The building is opened at night to test the new lighting, and over 13,000 persons visit the illuminated structure.

October 1, 1898. The Library is opened to the public in the evening on a regular basis.

December 25, 1898. The last of the 16 bronze portrait statues in the Main Reading Room is put into place.

January 14, 1899. A joint resolution is introduced in Congress authorizing the purchase of busts of Senators Morrill and Voorhees to commemorate "their constant efforts in forwarding the legislation for the construction of the Library of Congress."

August 9, 1902. Sculptor John Flanagan's clock over the entrance to the Main Reading Room is completed.

June 8, 1906. U.S. Court of Claims awards Smithmeyer & Pelz $159,864.63 for their design of the Library building.

1906. John L. Smithmeyer publishes *History of the Construction of the Library of Congress* in an attempt to persuade Congress to appropriate the sum awarded by the court.

May 22, 1908. Congress appropriates $320,000 to construct a stack in the southeast courtyard.

January 1910. The new southeast stack is completed and occupied.

January 23, 1925. Congress accepts a gift from Elizabeth Sprague Coolidge for the construction of an auditorium.

March 4, 1925. First appropriation for the construction of a stack in the northeast courtyard.

October 1925. Coolidge Auditorium completed in a portion of the northwest courtyard.

December 6, 1926. Librarian of Congress Herbert Putnam warns that, in spite of the pending completion of the new stack, additional space will be needed for the Library within a decade.

March 1927. Stack in the northeast courtyard is completed and occupied. Its total cost is $745,000.

June 13, 1930. Congress authorizes extension and remodeling of the east front of the building and appropriates $6,500,000 for the construction of an Annex Building.

1933. Extension of the east front is completed.

1938. The Annex Building is completed, and the transfer of materials out of the Main Building starts.

March 26, 1939. The Whittall Pavilion is opened.

October 12, 1939. The Hispanic Room is dedicated.

January 8, 1949. The Woodrow Wilson Room is dedicated.

April 23, 1951. The Poetry Room is dedicated.

June 27, 1956. Plaque honoring Senator Voorhees, who "took a leading part in obtaining this library building for the Amreican people," is placed in the staircase hall by the Business and Professional Women's Club of Covington, Indiana.

August 1958. Librarian of Congress L. Quincy Mumford proposes a third Library building.

May 4, 1964. The Main Reading Room is closed for cleaning and the installation of new lighting, heating, and ventilation systems, along with a new book-carrier system.

August 16, 1965. The Main Reading Room is reopened.

October 19, 1965. Congress authorizes the construction of a third Library structure, the James Madison Memorial Building.

April 24, 1980. The James Madison Memorial Building is dedicated.

June 13, 1980. The Annex Building is renamed the John Adams Building. The Main Building is renamed the Thomas Jefferson Building.

ℒAlbum

The progression of the first building for the Library of Congress from excavation to decoration is documented not only in Bernard R. Green's scrapbook and construction journal but in a remarkable series of photographs made for the architects and engineers. Of this extensive pictorial record, now in the Library's collections, the 13 pictures of construction work on the following pages are only a handful.

This photograph of the U.S. Capitol grounds was made by Levin C. Handy in the 1870's, when Carroll Row—the group of houses at the upper right—occupied the site that Congress purchased for the Library in 1886 at $2.56 a square foot. The statue on the east plaza of the Capitol is of George Washington; it was moved early in the 20th century to the Smithsonian Institution. LC–USP6–6544–A

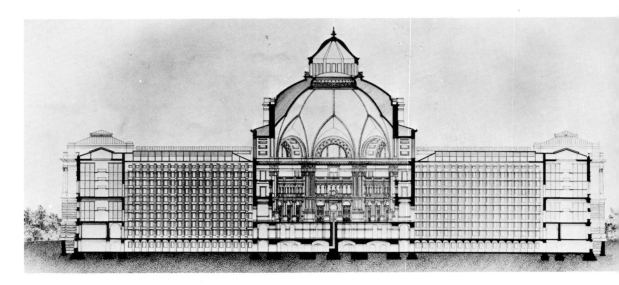

ARCH.'s OFFICE
CONG. LIB. BUILD'G
SEPT. 12TH 1888

Opposite page, top: *This cross-section drawing of the plan that won final approval from Congress in March 1889 depicts the interior of the central rotunda, the bookstacks flanking it, and the corner pavilions. Cutting across the building's center from north to south, it shows both similarities and differences when compared with the building that finally emerged. A great clock is shown above the Main Reading Room's entrance, for example, but its decorative sculpture is much simpler than the bronze sculpture that now adorns the clock above the entrance. LC–USP6–6504–A*

Opposite page, bottom: *June 8, 1888, when the land stood empty, uprooted, waiting for the miracle of a great building.*

Workmen had begun clearing the site for the Library Building Commission in late 1886, and the main excavations were complete in August 1887. Work stopped until February 1888 for the architect's cement tests. When this picture was taken, Mr. Smithmeyer was still architect, and Mr. Green had been superintendent of construction for two months. LC–USP6–6507–A

Above: *The excavation three months later. Congress placed the Army's Chief of Engineers in charge of the building three weeks after this picture was taken. LC–USP6–6508–A*

Opposite page, top: *By May 12, 1890, the massive structure had taken recognizable forms. The outlines of the design—a central rotunda and four courtyards surrounded by the north and south stacks and by the exterior wings of the building—can be seen here. Worksheds appear in the southwest, northwest, and northeast courts. LC–USP6–6510–A*

Opposite page, bottom: *The entire construction site, hidden from sidewalk superintendents by the fence, could be seen in all its immensity from the Capitol dome. The walls of the first level were up for this picture of July 30, 1890, revealing their rows of windows. Librarian Ainsworth Rand Spofford remarked upon the "great number of windows (nearly two thousand in all)" in his lectures about the building. He described the outer walls as "white granite, the whitest and purest known, from the quarries at Concord, New Hampshire. . . ." LC–USP6–6545–A*

Below: *The larger of the two modified plans submitted to Congress in late 1888 by Brig. Gen. Thomas L. Casey was approved on March 2, 1889, less than three months before this scene was recorded. The concrete foundation was completed by September 14 of that year. LC–USP6–6509–A*

CORNER
STONE

Above: *The cornerstone was laid at 3 p.m. on August 28, 1890, apparently without greater formality than a photograph for the record. A framed copy that undoubtedly hung in Mr. Green's office identifies the gentleman with the white beard (second from right) as Tom Broderick, head rigger, and the one in the derby hat and shirt sleeves as Ned Casey, foreman of laborers. No others are named, but the man at the right is reputed to be Mr. Green. LC–USP6–2232–A*

Opposite page, top: *This view of the northeast courtyard shows the third level in progress on January 7, 1891. Each court has a tower containing a circular staircase. Mr. Spofford described the walls of the four inner courts as built of "Maryland granite, of a slightly darker hue, from the quarries in Baltimore County" and "enameled brick of the color of ivory or porcelain. . . ." LC–USP6–6511–A*

Opposite page, bottom: *The outer walls, more complex of design and execution, rose more slowly, as this view of the west front on May 22, 1891, shows. "The walls are sixty-nine feet high to the roof," said Mr. Spofford, "and the apex of the dome one hundred and ninety-five feet from the ground. The order of architecture is the Italian Renaissance, the central front and four corner pavilions being moderately projected, thus relieving the monotony of so long a façade." LC–USP6–6512–A*

Opposite page, top: *This view of the south front on August 27, 1891, shows the keystone heads at the top of the second story windows on the southwest pavilion walls. "The solid massiveness of the granite walls is relieved not only by the numerous windows, with their casings treated in high relief," Mr. Spofford pointed out, "but by foliated carvings beneath the cornices and pediments." LC–USP6–6515–A*

Opposite page, bottom: *"Next to the Reading Room,"* said Mr. Spofford, *"there opens out on either side an extensive book . . . repository, filled with cases of iron, consisting of nine tiers or floors, rising sixty-five feet high to the roof. . . . The shelves are constructed of bars of rolled steel . . . with a coating of magnetic oxide, which renders them as smooth as glass, and they are so spaced as to afford ample ventilation for*

the books and prevent any accumulation of dust. These shelves are adjustable to any height."

On September 1, 1892, the day before this picture was taken, Mr. Green wrote in his construction journal: "Finished cleaning down and pointing all of Book-stack walls, down to cellar." The scaffold in the Main Reading Room can be seen through the semicircular window. LC–USP6–6517–A

Above: *Not only was the third story of the outer walls underway on November 25, 1892, but the scaffold in the Octagon can be seen protruding where the dome would later appear. Six days before this view from the Capitol was recorded, Mr. Green wrote in his journal: "Scaffold up in O. to receive the dome ring." LC–USP6–6516–A*

Right: *On May 20, 1893, Mr. Green noted in his journal: "Ironwork of dome frame still in progress but now nearly finished. Should have been entirely done not later than April 15 last." On May 26 he wrote: "Began putting terra cotta on dome roof, starting with the lantern crown." On May 31, the day this picture was taken: "Finished terra cotta covering of lantern crown.—Ironwork of exterior shell of dome nearly all painted, 2nd coat of red lead, and that of inner shell begun." The west main pavilion can be seen at the left, the southeast pavilion at the right.*
LC–USP6–6521–A

Opposite page, bottom: *The dome was gilded by November 14, 1893, and the last stone of the super-structure set in place July 7, 1894. The bronze doors for the main entrance were not yet ready when this photograph was made on May 22, 1895, but nine portrait busts had been mounted above the pediments of the portico windows at the front and sides of the west main pavilion. "The massive front staircase, with its fine granite balustrade, has underneath it a heavily arched porte-cochere for carriage entrance," said Mr. Spofford that year. "The base or lower story of the building is in rusticated or rock-faced stone. At the corners of all the pavilions the granite is relieved by vermiculated work, while the walls of the whole edifice in its upper stories are of smooth bush-hammered granite. . . . The dome is gilded by a thick coating of gold leaf, twenty-three carats fine, costing about $3,800, a much more permanent as well as more economical finish than painting, which must be frequently renewed." LC–USP6–6526–A*

Above: *When the Library of Congress was moved in 1897, its new building contained nearly a million items—books, manuscripts, maps, prints, periodicals. In phrases that could only have come from Mr. Green, Mr. Spofford said that it was made of 400,000 cubic feet of granite, 550,000 enameled brick, 24 million red brick, 3,000 tons of iron and steel, and 70,000 barrels of cement. From 150 to 300 men, besides those in the quarries and elsewhere, "have been constantly employed" upon it. "As many as 80,000 brick have been laid in a single day," he marveled. "Some of the granite blocks weigh as much as eighteen tons each, or over 36,000 pounds in a single stone."*

The miracle had been created. LC–USP6–6534–A

The Exhibition

Note: With a few exceptions, items in this exhibition are from the collections of the Library of Congress, and the checklist that follows gives the division which has custody of each original item.

Orders for photocopies of Library of Congress materials should be placed with the Photoduplication Service, Library of Congress, Washington, D.C. 20540. Negative numbers should be cited to identify the items ordered.

Several items are from the collections of other institutions or have been lent by individuals. In those entries for which negative numbers are cited, the Library's Photoduplication Service can also supply photoprints. When no negative number is listed, however, photocopies should be ordered from the institution cited in the entry.

The Library's Original Home

Conceived in the Continental Congress and created by the Sixth Congress of the new United States in 1800, the Library of Congress had various quarters in the U.S. Capitol until 1897. Although it was often called "the national library" in its fledgling years, the epithet expressed national pride more than reality for much of its first century. Not until the collections—overflowing their quarters—were moved to their spacious new building in 1897 could all the services of a national library be offered to Congress and the Nation.

But the Library's story, with its antecedents in the 1780's, is entwined in the Nation's history. Three of the Nation's founding statesmen had roles in its early annals.

It was Delegate James Madison, the future Father of the Constitution, who chaired a committee in late 1782 and early 1783 to consider a motion to buy books for Congressional reference. For his committee's report, he drew up a want-list of some 300 "indispensable" titles in law, history, politics, and geography. For lack of funds, the motion failed.

Delegates and, later, Members of the U.S. Congress used the books of the Library Company of Philadelphia and the New York Society Library whenever they met in those cities in 1774–1800. But in the spring of 1800, Congress faced the impending move of the United States Government from Philadelphia to the newly created District of Columbia. In legislation providing for the "removal and accommodation" of the Government, Congress by necessity voted $5,000 to purchase books and to furnish a "suitable apartment" for them in the Capitol Building. John Adams,

second President of the United States (1797–1801), signed his approval on the parchment that created the Library on April 24, 1800.

Congress was out of session when eleven hair trunks holding 740 volumes and a case of three maps arrived from London in 1801. Legislation begun late that year produced the Act of January 26, 1802, which formally organized the Library, provided for Presidential appointment of a Librarian, and established a Joint Committee on the Library. Thomas Jefferson, the third President (1801–9), who took a lively interest in the new Library, approved the act on that date.

The collections had grown to more than 3,000 volumes when the British Army—retaliating for the American destruction of Upper Canada's parliament buildings with their library and archives in 1813—fired the U.S. Capitol on August 24, 1814, and burned all but a few of the books. On January 30, 1815, James Madison, the fourth President (1809–17), approved the act of Congress which appropriated $23,950 to buy what was probably the country's finest private library: that of the great bookman and retired President at Monticello. Jefferson's library, collected over 50 years, changed the scope of the Library's collections from a narrow parliamentary one to the broad range from which a truly national library could grow.

Ten years later, fire begun by a candle in the Library's new quarters did little damage. But a third blaze—caused by a faulty flue beneath the floor—destroyed some 35,000 among 55,000 volumes on Christmas Eve of 1851. Congress called for fireproofing, and Architect of the Capitol Thomas U. Walter restored the quarters, by then in the west front of the Capitol, in a handsomely decorated "Iron Room."

Here Ainsworth Rand Spofford, a Cincinnati bookseller and newspaperman, came as Assistant Librarian in 1861 and was appointed sixth Librarian of Congress by President Abraham Lincoln as 1864 closed. By 1872, Spofford's effort to make the collections comprehensive had more than doubled them in size, making them the country's largest: 175,000 volumes. The great Copyright Act of 1870, which he had sought in order to secure copyright deposits for "our only national library," was already having its effects.

Spofford first proposed a separate Library building to Congress in 1872. As 1876 opened, he was piling books on the floor. Twenty years later, they numbered 740,000 volumes, plus some 18,000 newspaper volumes, 200,000 musical items, 250,000 graphic works, and 40,000 maps and charts, as well as some manuscripts and uncounted magazines. By gift, exchange, purchase, and copyright deposits, he had made the collections nationally significant in quality. But many items were stored in the Capitol's cellar or elsewhere. By February 1897, when *Harper's Weekly* depicted the white-haired Librarian and his readers amid the piles of books, the Iron Room was in chaos.

It was long past time to move.

1. *The Act of Congress, April 24, 1800, providing for the Federal Government's move to the District of Columbia and creating the Library of Congress*
Photograph of engrossed and signed manuscript
Two pages

National Archives and Records Service, Washington, D.C.

2. JOHN ADAMS (1735–1826)
Second President of the United States
By H. H. Houston after William Joseph Williams, ca. 1796–98
Stipple engraving, 38.0 x 27.0 cm
National Portrait Gallery
Smithsonian Institution, Washington, D.C.

3. *The Act of January 26, 1802, organizing the Library and providing for a Librarian of Congress*
Photograph of engrossed and signed manuscript
One page
National Archives and Records Service, Washington, D.C.

4. THOMAS JEFFERSON (1743–1826)
Third President of the United States
By David Edwin after Rembrandt Peale, ca. 1801
Stipple engraving, 54.0 x 40.7 cm
National Portrait Gallery
Smithsonian Institution, Washington, D.C.

5. *The Act of January 30, 1815, appropriating $23,950 to purchase the library of Thomas Jefferson*
Photograph of engrossed and signed manuscript
One page
National Archives and Records Service, Washington, D.C.

6. JAMES MADISON (1751–1836)
Fourth President of the United States
By David Edwin after Thomas Sully and Gilbert Stuart, 1810
Stipple engraving, 61.2 x 39.1 cm, trimmed
Prints and Photographs Division

7. *"A View of the Capitol of the United States after the Conflagration of the 24th August 1814."*
By William Strickland after George Munger, ca. 1814
Color engraving, 33.0 x 45.7 cm, trimmed
Prints and Photographs Division

8. *The Library of Congress in the U.S. Capitol Building*
Photograph of an engraving, ca. 1853
Prints and Photographs Division
Negative LC–USZ62–1818

9. *"Scene in the Old Congressional Library . . . Showing Present Congested Condition"*
Photograph of a drawing by W. Bengough, HARPER'S WEEKLY, February 27, 1897
Prints and Photographs Division
Negative LC–USZ62–3868

Congress Holds a Competition: 1873

In response to Librarian Spofford's first plea for a building to house and service the Library's riches, Congress held a competition to elicit architectural designs. The event —suggested initially by architect John L. Smithmeyer, then in charge of constructing public buildings in the South—attracted 28 entries.

The Act of Congress which authorized the competition on March 3, 1873, provided for a committee of three judges. Senator Timothy Otis Howe of Wisconsin, then Chairman of the Joint Committee on the Library, was its chairman. Serving with him was Senator Justin Smith Morrill of Vermont, Chairman of the Senate Committee on Public Buildings and Grounds. The third judge was Librarian Spofford, who set forth certain specifications to be met by competing architects. The building must be fireproof—with an iron interior and a stone exterior. It must have a central reading room at its core, and it must house 2 million volumes. The building's dome must be lower than that of the Capitol. And its dimensions must be 270 feet wide by 340 feet long.

Architect Smithmeyer formed a partnership with architect Paul J. Pelz of Washington, D.C., to enter the contest. Their design in the style of the Italian Renaissance won first prize ($1,500). Second prize ($1,000) went to Adolph E. Melander of Boston, Massachusetts. An entry by Schulze & Schoen & Cluss of New York and Washington placed third ($500), and $1,000 was divided among another 10 contestants.

The 1873 designs of Smithmeyer & Pelz, Melander, and several other entrants whose drawings are in the Library's architectural collections reflect the styles of the times. Viewers will find the individual styles of the architects reminiscent, too, of buildings they actually designed in various cities.

10. AINSWORTH RAND SPOFFORD (1825–1908)
    Sixth Librarian of Congress, 1864–97
    Photograph, undated, by L. C. Handy Studios, Washington, D.C.
    Brady-Handy Collection
    Prints and Photographs Division
    Negative LC–USZ62–23839

11. TIMOTHY OTIS HOWE (1816–1883)
    Chairman of the Joint Committee on the Library, 1873–79
    Photograph, undated, by C. M. Bell, Washington, D.C.
    Prints and Photographs Division
    Negative LC–USZ6–1049

12. JUSTIN SMITH MORRILL (1810–1898)
    Member of the Senate Committee on Public Buildings and Grounds, ca. 1867–97, Chairman, 1870–76
    Photograph, undated
    Brady-Handy Collection
    Prints and Photographs Division
    Negative LC–B8184–29320

13. *Perspective view of design*
    By Leon Beaver, Dayton, Ohio, 1873
    Photograph of pencil, ink, and wash drawing, 66.1 x 76.0 cm
    Prints and Photographs Division
    Negative LC–USZ62–63235

14. *Perspective view of design*
    By F. Schumann and P. C. Lautrup, Washington, D.C., 1873
    Photograph of ink-and-wash drawing, 24.8 x 43.0 cm
    Prints and Photographs Division
    Negative LC–USZ62–63208

15. *Perspective view of design*
    By Adolph E. Melander, Boston, Massachusetts, 1873
    Photograph of a heliotype, 19.8 x 34.3 cm
    Prints and Photographs Division
    Negative LC–USZ62–63210

16. *Interior design for the "Library of Congress Art Gallery"*
By Adolph E. Melander, Boston, Massachusetts, 1873
Photograph of ink drawing, 41.3 x 36.3 cm
Prints and Photographs Division
Negative LC–USZ62–63209

17. *Side and front elevations of design*
By F. W. Chandler, Washington, D.C., 1873
Photograph of ink-and-wash drawing, 61.0 x 70.7 cm
Prints and Photographs Division
Negative LC–USZ62–63230

18. *Front elevation of design*
By E. G. Lind, Baltimore, Maryland, 1873
Photograph of ink drawing, 58.1 x 68.0 cm
Prints and Photographs Division
Negative LC–USZ62–63211

19. *Front elevation of design*
By Samuel Sloan, Philadelphia, Pennsylvania, 1873
Photograph of ink drawing, 37.8 x 66.0 cm
Prints and Photographs Division
Negative LC–USZ62–63197

20. *Side and front elevations of design*
By Alonzo B. Jones, Philadelphia, Pennsylvania, 1873
Photograph of ink drawing, 47.1 x 72.8 cm
Prints and Photographs Division
Negative LC–USZ62–59058

21. *Front and side elevations of design*
By Thomas U. Walter, Philadelphia, Pennsylvania, 1873
Photograph of ink drawing, 58.0 x 75.8 cm

Prints and Photographs Division
Negative LC–USZ62–63193

22. *Perspective view of design*
By Frederic H. Bicknell, Somerville, Massachusetts, 1873
Photograph of ink drawing, 49.4 x 74.1 cm
Prints and Photographs Division
Negative LC–USZ62–63239

23. *Front elevation of design*
By S. A. Fite, Philadelphia, Pennsylvania, 1873
Photograph of ink drawing, 27.6 x 57.0 cm
Prints and Photographs Division
Negative LC–USZ62–63227

24. JOHN L. SMITHMEYER (1832–1908)
Architect
Photograph from John L. Smithmeyer, HISTORY OF THE CONSTRUCTION OF THE LIBRARY OF CONGRESS, WASHINGTON, D.C. (Washington, privately printed, 1906)
Prints and Photographs Division
Negative LC–USZ62–59295

25. PAUL JOHANNES PELZ (1841–1918)
Architect
Photograph, undated
Paul J. Pelz Papers
Manuscript Division
Negative LC–USZ62–46800

26. *Perspective view of the winning design*
By Smithmeyer & Pelz, Washington, D.C., 1873
Photograph of ink drawing, 45.4 x 81.0 cm, annotated by Senator Daniel W. Voorhees
Prints and Photographs Division
Negative LC–USZ62–3765

Alternative Designs: 1874-86

After touring Europe's national libraries in 1874, Senator Howe decided that the winning entry lacked sufficient grandeur for a growing power. He asked the architects for a much larger plan in "Victorian Gothic" style. Congress later supported this renewal of the competition. For more than a dozen years, no building was authorized.

For a location, Senator Howe first favored the site of the Botanic Garden southwest of the Capitol, where the ground proved unsuitable for such a structure, then the downtown site of Judiciary Square. Other Members favored a Capitol Hill site, other styles of architecture, or other solutions—such as extending the Capitol's wings, or enlarging its east front, or even—for a brief time in 1882—raising its dome to provide space near the rotunda.

Throughout, Senator Morrill was a firm advocate of a separate building and of a site on Capitol Hill. Also supporting a separate building was Senator Daniel Wolsey Voorhees of Indiana, who succeeded Senator Howe as Chairman of the Joint Committee on the Library in 1879, after the latter had failed of reelection to the Senate.

Meanwhile, 41 new designs had been submitted, either by fresh competitors, such as Alexander R. Esty of Framingham, Massachusetts, or by original entrants of the 1873 contest—notably Smithmeyer & Pelz. The latter pair met Senator Howe's request with their enlarged "Victorian Gothic" design of 1874 and later with a "Thirteenth Century Gothic" plan, both for Judiciary Square.

To all proposals, indeed, Smithmeyer & Pelz responded with alternative designs in various styles for one site or another during the years 1874–86. When Senator Howe abandoned Gothic styles as too costly to win Congressional agreement, they produced French, German, and "Modern" Renaissance designs, a Romanesque plan, and variations of their original Italian Renaissance design. They even produced a plan to enlarge the Capitol. Mercifully, that historic structure was spared by the skills of Senators Morrill and Voorhees.

Action came in 1886. Congress passed a bill introduced by Representative Otho Robards Singleton of Mississippi, then Chairman of the House Committee on the Library, to erect a separate building. Approved on April 15, it specified Capitol Hill as the location and settled on an 1885 Smithmeyer & Pelz version of their 1873 Renaissance design.

Like the designs from the 1873 competition, Esty's later plan and the alternative designs of Smithmeyer & Pelz illustrate what might have been in an age when many Americans looked to Europe for artistic standards.

27. DANIEL WOLSEY VOORHEES (1827–1897)
    Member of the Joint Committee on the Library, 1879–97, Chairman, 1879–81
    Photograph, undated
    Brady-Handy Collection
    Prints and Photographs Division
    Negative LC–USZ6–1050

28. OTHO ROBARDS SINGLETON (1814–1889)
    Member of the Joint Committee on the Library, 1883–87, Chairman of the House Library Committee, 1883–87
    Photograph, undated
    Brady-Handy Collection
    Prints and Photographs Division
    Negative LC–B8184–1030

29. *Design for "Facade of the Proposed National Library" in "Victorian Gothic" style*
    By Smithmeyer & Pelz, 1874
    Photograph of ink-and-wash drawing, 67.9 x 124.5 cm

Prints and Photographs Division
Negative LC–USZ62–46793

30. *Perspective view of design for "Proposed Congressional Library, Washington, D.C."*
By Alexander R. Esty, Framingham, Massachusetts
Photograph of ink drawing, 54.0 x 83.5 cm
Prints and Photographs Division
Negative LC–USZ62–59059

31. *Perspective of "Thirteenth Century Gothic Design" for Judiciary Square site*
By Smithmeyer & Pelz, 1874–80
Photograph from Smithmeyer, HISTORY OF THE CONSTRUCTION OF THE LIBRARY OF CONGRESS
Prints and Photographs Division
Negative LC–USZ62–46797

32. *"Plan for the Proposed National Library" in the "German Renaissance" style for Judiciary Square site*
By Smithmeyer & Pelz, 1874–80
Photograph of ink drawing, 50.2 x 92.2 cm
Prints and Photographs Division
Negative LC–USZ62–46796

33. *Front elevation of design in "French Renaissance" style for Capitol Hill site*
By Smithmeyer & Pelz, 1874–80
Photograph of ink drawing, 44.0 x 88.2 cm
Prints and Photographs Division
Negative LC–USZ62–46794

34. *Perspective view of "Plan for the Extension of the Capitol (with Introduction of Turrets)"*
By Smithmeyer & Pelz, 1880
Photograph from Smithmeyer, HISTORY OF THE CONSTRUCTION OF THE LIBRARY OF CONGRESS
Prints and Photographs Division
Negative LC–USZ62–46798

35. *Perspective view and plans for first and second floors of design for "Congressional Library"*
By Smithmeyer & Pelz, ca. 1881
Photograph from Smithmeyer, HISTORY OF THE CONSTRUCTION OF THE LIBRARY OF CONGRESS
Prints and Photographs Division
Negative LC–USZ62–059050

36. *Perspective view of design*
By Smithmeyer & Pelz, October 1885
Photograph of ink drawing, 60.8 x 132.4 cm
Prints and Photographs Division
Negative LC–USZ62–63170

37. *Front elevation of "Romanesque Design, Congressional Library," for site southwest of the Capitol*
By Smithmeyer & Pelz, 1874–86
Photograph from Smithmeyer, HISTORY OF THE CONSTRUCTION OF THE LIBRARY OF CONGRESS
Prints and Photographs Division
Negative LC–USZ62–63172

Design Changes and Excavation: 1886-88

In the 1886 act, Congress created a commission to acquire land at no more than $550,000 and to supervise the building project. Designated were the Secretary of the Interior as Chairman, the Librarian of Congress (Spofford), and the Architect of the Capitol (then Edward Clark). Former Senator Lucius Quintus Cincinnatus Lamar, Interior Secretary in 1885–88, was appointed to the Supreme Court in early 1888 and was succeeded by William Freeman Vilas, Interior Secretary in 1888–89.

Land south of East Capitol Street proved less costly than the present site of the Supreme Court to the north. Still, property owners won another $35,000 in a court suit on July 31, bringing the total cost of the land to $2.56 a square foot.

John L. Smithmeyer was appointed architect for the Library building in October 1886. Paul J. Pelz became assistant architect in November. Clearing of the site had begun in late October, but excavation proceeded slowly for having too many cooks in the architectural kitchen. Initial digging was at the site's southwest corner, where Clark favored situating the building; but Smithmeyer's choice of the present setting ultimately prevailed. Excavation was completed in August 1887. Then all work stopped until mid-February 1888, while Smithmeyer challenged the quality of a contractor's cement and proceeded to conduct 615 tests on various cements.

A House investigation of the delay followed (May-September 1888), amid public controversy. Meanwhile, on March 15, the commission had hired civil engineer Bernard Richardson Green to superintend construction. Chairman Vilas ended the cement problem with tests by the U.S. Army Engineers and trimmed Smithmeyer's payroll of nonessential employees. After the House hearings, marked by debate over building costs and animosity toward Smithmeyer, Congress resolved the controversy in an Act of October 2, 1888. The part-time commission, whose members all had other full-time jobs, was dissolved and Brig. Gen. Thomas Lincoln Casey, Chief of the Army Engineers, was placed in charge of the project, with Green as his superintendent. Congress provided funds for construction and instructed General Casey to submit a design limiting costs to $4 million.

The next day Smithmeyer was dismissed and Pelz promoted to architect. The drawing Pelz produced for General Casey that autumn removed the statues that had topped the corner pavilions in the 1885 design and in a September 1888 drawing. It removed two hexagonal domes from the 1888 design's main pavilion. And it decreased the exterior to 333 by 318 feet—limiting future book-storage capacity.

But a week after General Casey presented that $4 million design to Congress on November 23, 1888, he presented a second Pelz design, priced at $6 million. This design, looking much as the building looks today, also omitted the corner sculptures and the hexagonal domes; but its exterior dimensions were 470 feet by 338 feet, and its interior spaces repeated those of 1886. With it, General Casey presented Spofford's space needs.

Congress approved the $6 million plan on March 2, 1889, and construction went forward to completion in 1897. Some changes made in the interim can be seen by comparing Pelz' general plan of the building and grounds for the $6 million design with one that he signed in April 1892. The perspective view in a heliotype after a drawing by L. F. Graether depicts the building as executed and shows the rounding of the central dome.

38. LUCIUS QUINTUS CINCINNATUS LAMAR (1825–1893)
   Secretary of the Interior, 1885–88
   Photograph, undated
   Prints and Photographs Division
   Negative LC–USZ61–9441

39. WILLIAM FREEMAN VILAS (1840–1908)
   Secretary of the Interior, 1888–89
   Photograph, undated
   Prints and Photographs Division
   Negative LC–USZ62–19988

40. EDWARD CLARK (1824–1902)
   Architect of the Capitol, 1865–1902
   Photograph, undated
   Brady-Handy Collection
   Prints and Photographs Division
   Negative LC–B8184–4200

41. *Site of the Library's future building as seen from the Capitol, looking east down East Capitol Street*
   Photograph by L. C. Handy Studios, Washington, D.C., 1880
   Brady-Handy Collection
   Prints and Photographs Division
   Negative LC–USP6–6544–A

42. *Site of the Library's future building as seen from the Capitol looking southeast, with Pennsylvania Avenue on the right*
   Photograph by L. C. Handy Studios, Washington, D.C., 1880
   Brady-Handy Collection
   Prints and Photographs Division
   Negative LC–USZ62–12439

43. *View of excavation for the Library of Congress building*
   Photograph, June 8, 1888
   Prints and Photographs Division
   Negative LC–USP6–6507–A

44. *Perspective view of the "Design of the Congressional Library Building, Adopted by Act of Congress, Approved April 15, 1886"*
   By Smithmeyer and Pelz, September 1888
   Photograph of ink drawing, 53.5 x 74.3 cm
   Prints and Photographs Division
   Negative LC–USZ62–63167

45. *"View of One of the Corridors of First Story"*
   By H. Sill for Smithmeyer & Pelz, 1888
   Photograph of ink drawing, 62.1 x 51.6 cm
   Prints and Photographs Division
   Negative LC–USZ62–059055

46. *Perspective drawing of the Library's Great Hall*
   By Paul J. Pelz, March 1888
   Photograph of ink drawing, 53.1 x 50.3 cm
   Prints and Photographs Division
   Negative LC–USP6–6505–A

47. *"Design for Building for the Library of Congress Prepared in Accordance with Act of Congress Approved October 2, 1888"*
   By Paul J. Pelz, November 1888
   Photograph of ink-and-wash drawing, 73.1 x 78.6 cm
   Prints and Photographs Division
   Negative LC–USZ62–59056

48. *Section drawing of the "Building for the Library of Congress Adopted by Act of Congress Approved April 15, 1886"*
   By Paul J. Pelz, November, 1888
   Photograph of ink-and-wash drawing, 70.9 x 96.4 cm
   Prints and Photographs Division
   Negative LC–USZ62–63166

49. *Perspective view of "Building for the Library of Congress, View from the South-West"*
   By Paul J. Pelz, November 1888
   Photograph of pen-and-ink drawing
   Prints and Photographs Division
   Negative LC–USZ62–59282

50. *View of "General Plan" for Library of Congress building and grounds*
   By Paul J. Pelz, November 1888
   Photograph of ink-and-water-color drawing, 73.6 x 96.4 cm
   Prints and Photographs Division
   Negative LC–USZ62–59048

51. *Perspective view of the "Building of the Library of Congress, View from Senate Wing of Capitol"*
   Photograph of a heliotype after a drawing by L. F. Graether
   Prints and Photographs Division
   Negative LC–USZ62–59283

52. *View of "General Plan of Streets & Approaches"*
   Drawn by L. F. Graether and signed by Paul J. Pelz, April 1892
   Photograph of pencil, ink, and wash drawing, 65.2 x 109.4 cm
   Prints and Photographs Division
   Negative LC–USZ62–63165

Construction: 1889-97

General Casey's overall direction of the Library building's construction was a Congressional assignment in addition to his other projects as Chief of the Army Engineers. Green's post as superintendent of construction was a full-time job. Joining this team in December 1892 was the general's young son, architect Edward Pearce Casey, who supervised the interior designs for the remainder of the project, advised on the artistic decorations, and later supplied designs for furnishings.

General Casey's widely acclaimed efficiency and ability to manage costs were shared by his superintendent. Upon the general's death in 1896, Congress placed Green in charge almost at once. By February 1897, practical construction was complete. Several works of art and two book-carriers were not yet on hand, but Green included their cost in his detailed report of April 22, 1897, on expenditures made since General Casey had taken charge on October 2, 1888, which totaled $6,090,153.28. In addition, the 1886–88 commission had spent $254,432.06 to clear, enclose, excavate, and drain the site and to prepare plans, bringing total construction costs to $6,344,585.34. Meanwhile, by an Act of February 19, 1897, Congress had terminated Green's post as of March 4 and directed him to serve as Superintendent of the Building and Grounds, four months before his Presidential appointment to that post.

In the intervening years, Green had been an extraordinary documentalist. His journals on the construction and decoration of the building animate its history and enliven the annual reports to Congress and other official records.

Even more fascinating is the Library's splendid collection of the official photographs that documented progress year by year, at times month by month. Created on glass plates, many of which have eroded with time, these images are preserved also as prints, and a number have been copied in succeeding years. They depict with great clarity the work of creating a miracle in stone and steel.

Of curious note are two pictures for which the time of day as well as the date have been recorded. The one taken at 3 P.M. on August 28, 1890, has always been celebrated as the photograph depicting the laying of the building's cornerstone. Green himself reported it as such in a memorandum dated August 28, 1890: "On this day at three o'clock, the chief cornerstone of the superstructure of the Building for the Library of Congress was laid without ceremony as shown by the enclosed photograph of the operation."

He had planned in early May 1980 to lay the stone "in the regular course of construction and without special ceremony," but a Joint Resolution introduced in the House of Representatives on May 17 had called for "suitable Masonic ceremonies under the management of the Joint Committee on the Library in co-operation with the Chief of Engineers of the United States Army." The engineers deferred the setting of the stone and awaited action. None came—"the resolution having been informally laid aside for this Session. . . ." To avoid serious delay in construction, "it has become necessary to place the stone in position."

In a cavity of the stone, the engineers placed a copper box, 9½ by 6½ by 3½ inches in size and hermetically sealed. In it were the 1872 *Annual Report of the Librarian of Congress,* in which Spofford first proposed a separate building, and his 1888 report; General Casey's annual reports on the building for 1888 and 1889; a sealed glass tube containing photographs of a perspective drawing of the building from the southwest and of work progress on August 15, 1890; a synopsis of events relating to the building in 1866–90; the latest edition of the *Congressional Directory* (May 10 1890) ; the *American Almanac* for 1889; two Washington newspapers, the *Evening Star* of August 27 and the *Washington Post* of August 28, 1890, and two New York newspapers, the *Tribune* and the *World* of August 28, 1890. No date was inscribed on the cornerstone at the time. In 1952, the date was added to the stone's north face by the Architect of the Capitol.

The northeast pavilion is at a rear corner of the building. The cornerstone of the northwest pavilion at the front was laid in the regular course of construction at 3:10 P.M. on November 25, 1889, as shown in the photograph inscribed with that date. Congress was not in session at the time.

53. THOMAS LINCOLN CASEY (1831–1896)
    Chief of the Army Engineers, 1888–96
    Photograph from THE CASEY FAMILY OF EAST GREENWICH . . . (East Greenwich, R.I., 1927)
    Courtesy Daughters of the American Revolution Library
    Photoduplication Service files
    Negative LC–USP6–6502–C

54. BERNARD RICHARDSON GREEN (1843–1914)
    Superintendent of Construction, 1888–97
    Photograph, undated
    Photoduplication Service files
    Negative LC–USP6–6496–A

55. *"Journal of Operations on the Building for the Library of Congress," October 1888–August 1902*
    By Bernard Richardson Green
    Manuscript, 2 vols.
    Manuscript Division

56. EDWARD PEARCE CASEY (1864–1940)
    Architect
    Photograph from THE CASEY FAMILY OF EAST GREENWICH
    Courtesy Daughters of the American Revolution Library

Photoduplication Service files
Negative LC–USP6–6501–C

57. *View of foundation, looking toward Capitol*
    Photograph, 1889
    Prints and Photographs Division
    Negative LC–USZ62–73535

58. *Excavation work in progress*
    Photograph, June 26, 1889
    Prints and Photographs Division
    Negative LC–USP6–6509–A

59. *Laying the cornerstone of the northwest pavilion*
    Photograph, November 25, 1889
    Prints and Photographs Division
    Negative LC–USZ62–73536

60. *Brickmasons at work on the foundation*
    Photograph, November 1889
    Prints and Photographs Division
    Negative LC–USZ62–73540

61. *Testing the weight-bearing capacity of the basement floor arch*
    Photograph, June 19, 1890
    Prints and Photographs Division
    Negative LC–USZ62–73541

62. *View of the construction site from the Capitol*
    Photograph, July 30, 1890
    Prints and Photographs Division
    Negative LC–USP6–6545–A

63. *Laying the cornerstone of the northeast pavilion*
    Photograph, August 28, 1890
    Prints and Photographs Division
    Negative LC–USZ62–73542

64. *View of the southwest corner and west main pavilion*
    Photograph, August 27, 1891
    Prints and Photographs Division
    Negative LC–USZ62–59279

65. *Exterior walls of the north stack, looking toward the Capitol*
    Photograph, December 4, 1891
    Prints and Photographs Division
    Negative LC–USZ62–59151

66. *View of the construction site from the Capitol*
    Photograph, November 25, 1892
    Prints and Photographs Division
    Negative LC–USP6–6516–A

67. *View of the superstructure taking form above the rotunda*
    Photograph, May 10, 1893
    Prints and Photographs Division
    Negative LC–USZ62–73543

68. *Iron framework of the dome's superstructure*
    Photograph, April 19, 1893
    Prints and Photographs Division
    Negative LC–USZ62–73545

69. *View of the dome during gilding of the lantern*
    Photograph, September 5, 1893
    Prints and Photographs Division
    Negative LC–USZ62–73544

70. *View of the west façade showing the rotunda's gilded lantern*
Photograph, July 7, 1894
Prints and Photographs Division
Negative LC–USP6–6522–A

71. *View of the completed Library of Congress building from the Capitol grounds*
Photograph, undated
Prints and Photographs Division
Negative LC–USP6–6534–A

72. *View of the Library of Congress from the U.S. Capitol*
Photograph, 1898
Prints and Photographs Division
Negative LC–USZ6–1102

73. *West façade of the new Library building*
Photograph, 1898
Prints and Photographs Division
Negative LC–USZ6–1103

74. *View from the Library's main plaza, looking toward the U.S. Capitol*
Color photograph, 1980
Prints and Photographs Division
Negative LC–USZ6–1072

For additional related items, see the Slide Show : Constructing the Building, pages 94–95

Drawings for the Engineers

Hundreds of architectural drawings depict the multitudinous details of structure and decoration involved in creating such an ornate and massive building. Some bear the signature of architect Paul J. Pelz, and many are stamped with the seal of architect Edward Pearce Casey's New York office. These drawings not only guided the engineers who erected the structure in the 1890's, but they have also served throughout the years and remain today as the reference tools for the building's continuing maintenance. Even the few drawings selected for display astound the mind with the variety of detail required of the building's creators.

75. *"Stucco Work of W. Curtain Corridors and the Stucco and Marble Work of Vestibule, S.W. Pav[ilion], First Story"*
Photograph of ink drawing, 70.0 x 93.5 cm
Library of Congress Archives, Central Services Division
Negative LC–USZ6–1073

76. *"Finish of Librarian's Office, W. M., First Story. Sections and Elevations"*
Photograph of ink drawing, 76.0 x 102.5 cm
Library of Congress Archives, Central Services Division
Negative LC–USZ6–1074

77. *"Congressional [Senate] Reading Room, S.W. P[avilion,] First Story. Mantel and Side Elevations"*
Photograph of ink drawing, 69.5 x 96 cm
Library of Congress Archives, Central Services Division
Negative LC–USZ6–1075

78. *"Bronze Doors, Main Entrance, W. M. [Pavilion]"*
Photograph of ink drawing, 71.0 x 98.0 cm
Library of Congress Archives, Central Services Division
Negative LC–USZ6–1076

79. *"Plaster and Stucco Work. Reading Room, Dome, & Lantern"*
Photograph of ink drawing, 111.8 x 94.0 cm
Library of Congress Archives, Central Services Division
Negative LC–USZ6–1077

80. *"Ornamental Sheet Copper Work with its Supporting Framework. General Details, Dome and Lantern"*
Photograph of ink drawing, 73.0 x 125.5 cm
Library of Congress Archives, Central Services Division
Negative LC–USZ6–1078

81. *"Lamps and Posts for Approaches"*
Photograph of ink drawing, 61.5 x 95.0 cm
Library of Congress Archives, Central Services Division
Negative LC–USZ6–1079

82. *"Woodwork. Full Size Details of Telephone Closets, Reading Room"*
Photograph of ink drawing, 74.0 x 102.0 cm
Library of Congress Archives, Central Services Division
Negative LC–LSZ6–1080

83. *"Ironwork, General Drawing of Construction of Dome"*
Photograph of ink drawing, 81.0 x 134.0 cm
Library of Congress Archives, Central Services Division
Negative LC–USZ6–1081

84. *"Marblework. Tile and Mosaic Floor, West Corridors, First Story"*
Photograph of ink drawing, 71.0 x 104.0 cm
Library of Congress Archives, Central Services Division
Negative LC–USZ6–1082

85. *"Detail. Elevation of Wall Back of Colonnade, 2nd Story"*
Photograph of ink drawing, 71.5 x 105.5 cm
Library of Congress Archives, Central Services Division
Negative LC–USZ6–1083

86. *"Detail of Attic. Main Building Front"*
Photograph of ink drawing, 68.0 x 106.5 cm
Library of Congress Archives, Central Services Division
Negative LC–USZ6–1084

American Artists Create a Masterpiece

To the stranger's eye, so many works of art amid the profusion of lavish decorations are overwhelming at first glance. Symbols abound wherever one looks. To study their meanings, to sort out the decorative designs, or merely to read the numerous inscriptions takes time. But the eye is never bored.

More than a hundred mural paintings adorn the tympanums and the vaulted ceilings of the west main pavilion, the corner pavilions, and the western curtains. Two more in the lantern and the collar of the rotunda's dome look down on 24 statues and the magnificent sculpture surmounting the great clock. On the building's exterior are 42 granite sculptures in addition to the reliefs on the bronze doors and in their granite spandrels. Dominating the western view of the exterior is the "Fountain of Neptune."

Most of these works symbolize some aspect of civilization. Favorite themes are learning and knowledge—stressing the arts and sciences in particular—the means of transmitting knowledge, and society and its structure—the family and government. Some paintings represent myths and legends celebrated in literature, and nature and her seasons are represented in both paintings and bas-reliefs. Some murals are didactic—notably Elihu Vedder's five murals on "Government," in which the artist contrasts corrupt government, leading to anarchy, with good government, leading to peace and prosperity. In the rotunda, the lantern's mural represents human understanding, and the painting in the collar of the dome symbolizes the contributions of other civilizations to the American heritage.

Twenty-four statues dominate the Visitors' Gallery—eight symbolizing civilized activities and sixteen portraying outstanding figures in those endeavors. On the exterior, nine more such portraits appear in the granite busts on the west main pavilion's portico. As keystones for the windows of the corner pavilions, 33 ethnological heads based on anthropological studies of the 1890's symbolize the peoples of the world.

Because the larger works of art dominate, many of the decorative designs and symbols escape attention at first view. Each time the observant visitor—or staff member—walks through the marble halls, he discovers some imaginative, often playful detail in the ornamentation. Lively fishes and exotic birds can be found in the capitals of the columns in the galleries surrounding the well, or staircase hall, of the Great Hall. The signs of the zodiac among the brass inlays in the floor of that hall are obvious, but the symbols of the various occupations of humankind require study of the cherubs on the staircase railings. High above, in the cove beneath the six skylights, are symbols of the same theme—a palette and brushes, a sculptor's tool, books, Pan's pipes, cymbals, a lyre, a trumpet, a guitar, a scythe, a compass, and others.

In the vaulted mosaic ceilings are printer's marks, emblems of the arts and sciences, and names famous for creativity. The coffered ceilings of the western curtains and corner pavilions differ in design from the rotunda's coffered dome. And in the dome's stucco ornamentation are symbols of both myth and nature—griffins and tridents and winged geniuses among sea horses, dolphins, eagles, storks, and shells.

Apart from the artists commissioned for individual works, seven artists under architect Edward Pearce Casey's general supervision carried out the ornamental designs. Elmer E. Garnsey was in charge of the color decoration in the interior and had a staff of designers and fresco painters headed by Edward J. Holslag. William A. Mackay and Frederick C. Martin carried out the finer portions of the wall designs. W. Mills Thompson and Charles Caffin made the finished cartoons for some 25 fresco painters. In charge of the stucco ornamentation was Albert Weinert, whose staff of modelers executed the relief arabesques and minor sculptures.

The entirety became and remains astounding. Never before had the United States Government commissioned so many works of art for a public building or decorated a building so sumptuously. It could have happened, perhaps, only in that era when the decorative arts flourished so popularly.

In the 20th century, until the recent revival of interest in the artists whose works grace the Library and many another building across the land, new schools of art dimmed the Nation's memory of these painters, designers, and sculptors. But the Library's works of art and decoration, in their total effect, have never ceased to fascinate the public. The artists had indeed created a masterpiece.

87. *"Fresco Decoration of Vault, W. M. [Pavilion], East. 2nd Story"*
    Photograph of ink drawing, 77.0 x 104.5 cm
    Library of Congress Archives, Central Services Division
    Negative LC–USZ6–1085

88. *"Ornamental Iron Work, Stacks"*
    Photograph of ink drawing, 72.5 x 103.0 cm
    Library of Congress Archives, Central Services Division
    Negative LC–USZ6–1086

Painters, Sculptors, and Designers

Most of the 52 artists who were either commissioned for specific works of art or hired for a time to create decorative designs were relatively young in the 1890's. Although four were born in the 1830's and nine in the 1840's, the others were children of the sixties and seventies. The press proudly proclaimed that all were American artists, and indeed the group included both native and immigrant Americans. Most had studied abroad, and many were good friends who had already worked together on various other projects.

Although illustrations of the works of many of these artists are easily found in the publications of their day, portraits of the artists themselves are more difficult to find. Portraits of the following could not be located in time for this exhibition: the sculptor William Boyd, designer Charles Caffin, sculptor John Donoghue, and painters Carl Gutherz, Edward J. Holslag, William Andrew Mackay, Frederick C. Martin, Charles Sprague Pearce, Robert Reid, Herman T. Schladermundt, W. Mills Thompson, and William B. Van Ingen.

89. HERBERT ADAMS (1856–1945)
    Sculptor
    Photograph, 1918
    Prints and Photographs Division
    Negative LC–USZ62–73537

90. JOHN WHITE ALEXANDER (1856–1915)
    Painter
    Photograph from HARPER'S NEW MONTHLY MAGAZINE, May 1900
    General collections
    Negative LC–USZ6–1056

91. GEORGE RANDOLPH BARSE (1861–1938)
    Painter
    Photograph from NATIONAL CYCLOPEDIA OF BIOGRAPHY (New York, Jas. T. White & Co., 1940)
    General collections
    Negative LC–USZ6–1057

92. PAUL WAYLAND BARTLETT (1865–1925)
    Sculptor
    Photograph by Underwood and Underwood, undated
    Prints and Photographs Division
    Negative LC–USZ6–1051

93. THEODORE BAUER (dates unknown)
    Sculptor
    Photograph, undated
    Brady-Handy Collection
    Prints and Photographs Division
    Negative LC–USZ62–73707

94. FRANK WESTON BENSON (1862–1951)
Painter
Photograph, undated
Archives of American Art
Smithsonian Institution, Washington, D.C.

95. GEORGE EDWIN BISSELL (1839–1920)
Sculptor
Photograph from NATIONAL CYCLOPEDIA OF AMERI-
CAN BIOGRAPHY (New York, Jas. T. White & Co.,
1924)
General collections
Negative LC–USZ6–1058

96. EDWIN HOWLAND BLASHFIELD (1848–1936)
Painter
Photograph by Pirie MacDonald, New York, 1915
Prints and Photographs Division
Negative LC–USZ62–73538

97. JOHN J. BOYLE (1852–1902)
Sculptor
Photograph from 26th ANNUAL REPORT OF THE FAIR-
MOUNT PARK ART ASSOCIATION (Philadelphia, Pa.,
1898)
General collections
Negative LC–USZ6–1059

98. KENYON COX (1856–1919)
Painter
Photograph by Pirie MacDonald, New York, 1906
Prints and Photographs Division
Negative LC–USZ62–73539

99. CYRUS EDWIN DALLIN (1861–1944)
Sculptor
Photograph from NEW ENGLAND MAGAZINE, AN IL-
LUSTRATED MONTHLY, October 1899
General collections
Negative LC–USZ6–1060

100. FREDERICK DIELMAN (1847–1935)
Painter
Photograph by White Studio, New York, undated
Patten Collection
Prints and Photographs Division
Negative LC–USZ62–73546

101. ROBERT LEFTWICH DODGE (ca. 1872–1940)
Painter
Photograph, undated
Courtesy Mrs. Sara Dodge Kimbrough, Bay St.
Louis, Mississippi

102. WILLIAM DE LEFTWICH DODGE (1867–1935)
Painter
Photograph, ca. 1925–30
Courtesy Mrs. Sara Dodge Kimbrough, Bay St.
Louis, Mississippi

103. HENRY JACKSON ELLICOTT (1847–1901)
Sculptor
Photograph of a drawing from NATIONAL CYCLO-
PEDIA OF AMERICAN BIOGRAPHY (New York, Jas.
T. White & Co., 1904)
General collections
Negative LC–USZ6–1061

104. JOHN FLANAGAN (1865–1952)
Sculptor
Photograph from COSMOPOLITAN, AN ILLUSTRATED
MONTHLY MAGAZINE, May 1900
General collections
Negative LC–USZ6–1062

105. DANIEL CHESTER FRENCH (1850–1931)
Sculptor
Photograph by Pirie MacDonald, New York, 1913
Prints and Photographs Division
Negative LC–USZ62–73548

106. ELMER ELLSWORTH GARNSEY (1862–1946)
Painter
Photograph from NATIONAL CYCLOPEDIA OF AMERI-
CAN BIOGRAPHY (New York, Jas. T. White & Co.,
1949)
General collections
Negative LC–USZ6–1063

107. JONATHAN SCOTT HARTLEY (1845–1912)
Sculptor
Photograph from NATIONAL CYCLOPEDIA OF AMERI-
CAN BIOGRAPHY (New York, Jas. T. White & Co.,
1953)
General collections
Negative LC–USZ6–1064

108. WALTER McEWEN (1860–1943)
Painter
Photograph from NATIONAL CYCLOPEDIA OF AMERI-
CAN BIOGRAPHY (New York, Jas. T. White & Co.,
1916
General collections
Negative LC–USZ6–1065

109. FREDERICK WILLIAM MACMONNIES (1863–1937)
Sculptor
Photograph by Pirie MacDonald, New York, 1918
Prints and Photographs Division
Negative LC–USZ62–73549

110. PHILIP MARTINY (1858–1927)
Sculptor
Photograph, undated
Courtesy Robert Martiny, Sunnyside, New York,
and Raymond Linder, Huntington, Long Island,
New York

111. GEORGE WILLOUGHBY MAYNARD (1843–1923)
Sculptor
Photograph, undated
Division of Photographic History
Museum of History and Technology
Smithsonian Institution, Washington, D.C.

112. JULIUS GARI MELCHERS (1860–1932)
Painter
Photograph, undated
Division of Photographic History
Museum of History and Technology
Smithsonian Institution, Washington, D.C.

113. CHARLES HENRY NIEHAUS (1855–1935)
Sculptor
Photograph from MONTHLY ILLUSTRATOR AND HOME AND COUNTRY, June 1896
General collections
Negative LC–USZ6–1066

114. ROLAND HINTON PERRY (1870–1941)
Sculptor
Photograph, undated
Archives of American Art
Smithsonian Institution, Washington, D.C.

115. EDWARD CLARK POTTER (1857–1923)
Sculptor
Photograph, undated
Prints and Photographs Division
Negative LC–USZ6–1054

116. BELA LYON PRATT (1867–1917)
Sculptor
Photograph from NEW ENGLAND MAGAZINE, February 1903
General collections
Negative LC–USZ6–1067

117. FREDERICK WELLINGTON RUCKSTUHL (1853–1942)
Sculptor
Photograph from NEW ENGLAND MAGAZINE, February 1902
General collections
Negative LC–USZ6–1068

118. AUGUSTUS ST. GAUDENS (1848–1907)
Sculptor
Photograph, undated
Division of Photographic History
Museum of History and Technology
Smithsonian Institution, Washington, D.C.

119. LOUIS ST. GAUDENS (1854–1913)
Sculptor
Photograph of a clay bust by Annette J. St. Gaudens, ca. 1913–14
Courtesy St. Gaudens National Historic Site, National Park Service, U.S. Department of the Interior

120. WALTER SHIRLAW (1838–1909)
Painter
Photograph, undated
Division of Photographic History
Museum of History and Technology
Smithsonian Institution, Washington, D.C.

121. EDWARD EMERSON SIMMONS (1852–1931)
Painter
Photograph, undated
Prints and Photographs Division
Negative LC–USZ6–1055

122. FRANÇOIS MICHEL LOUIS TONETTI-DOZZI (1863–1920)
Sculptor
Photograph of a portrait by François Flameng, 1911

Courtesy Historical Society of Rockland County, New York, and Joseph L. Tonetti, Snedens Landing, New York

123. ELIHU VEDDER (1836–1923)
Painter
Photograph from NEW ENGLAND MAGAZINE, April 1896
General collections
Negative LC–USZ6–1069

124. HENRY OLIVER WALKER (1843–1929)
Painter
Photograph from NATIONAL CYCLOPEDIA OF AMERICAN BIOGRAPHY (New York, Jas. T. White & Co., 1932)
General collections
Negative LC–USZ6–1071

125. JOHN QUINCY ADAMS WARD (1830–1910)
Sculptor
Photograph from Adeline Adams, JOHN QUINCY ADAMS WARD, AN APPRECIATION (New York, 1922)
General collections
Negative LC–USZ6–1070

126. OLIN LEVI WARNER (1844–1896)
Sculptor
Photograph, undated
Courtesy George Gurney, Washington, D.C.

Ornamentation

Among the official photographs that were taken to record the progress of construction is a group depicting a few of the decorations at early stages. Among them, too, are pictures of Superintendent Green's rotating or "traveling" scaffold for the decoration of the interior dome.

Evidence that changes were made as decoration progressed can be seen in two pictures of the models for the granite sculptures in the spandrels of the three arches at the main entrance to the west main pavilion. The models for "Science" and "Literature" show a much more elaborate design for the keystones than the one adopted and depicted in the third sculpture, "Art."

127. *Sculpted marble in the northeast curtain of the main floor*
Photograph, October 16, 1894
Prints and Photographs Division
Negative LC–USP6–6524–A

128. *Marble carvers at work in a temporary workshed on the construction site*

Photograph, August 8, 1891
Prints and Photographs Division
Negative LC–USP6–6630–A

129. *Stucco shop in the north curtain, second floor*
Photograph, July 19, 1894
Prints and Photographs Division
Negative LC–USP6–6643–A

130. *Model for the granite sculpture "Literature"*
By Bela Lyon Pratt
Photograph, ca. 1894–95
Prints and Photographs Division
Negative LC–USP6–8645–A

131. *Model for the granite sculpture "Science"*
By Bela Lyon Pratt
Photograph, 1894
Prints and Photographs Division
Negative LC–USZ6–73600

132. *Granite sculpture "Art"*
By Bela Lyon Pratt
Photograph, 1895
Prints and Photographs Division
Negative LC–USZ6–1087

133. *Stucco elements for vaulted ceiling*
Photograph, ca. 1894–96
Prints and Photographs Division
Negative LC–USZ62–73560

134. *Section of dome ceiling showing stucco ornamentation*
Photograph, ca. 1895–96
Prints and Photographs Division
Negative LC–USP6–6530–A

135. *Blind window designed for the corner pavilions*
Photograph, undated
Prints and Photographs Division
Negative LC–USZ62–73601

136. *Corinthian capital for the Main Reading Room*
Photograph, ca. 1894–96
Prints and Photographs Division
Negative LC–USZ62–73561

137. *Sculpted corbel in the Great Hall*
Photograph from MONOGRAPHS OF AMERICAN ARCHITECTURE, vol. 6 (Boston, Ticknor, 1898)
Prints and Photographs Division
Negative LC–USZ62–47259

138. *Rotating scaffold designed by Bernard Richardson Green for the Main Reading Room*
Photograph, October 18, 1894
Prints and Photographs Division
Negative LC–USZ62–73566

139. *View of interior of dome showing partially completed stucco work*
Photograph, October 18, 1894
Prints and Photographs Division
Negative LC–USZ62–73565

140. *Rotating scaffold in the Main Reading Room*
Photograph from SCIENTIFIC AMERICAN, November 14, 1896

Photoduplication Service files
Negative LC–USP6–6529–A

141. *Partly completed mural "The Evolution of Civilization"*
By Edwin Howland Blashfield
Photograph, ca. 1895–96
Prints and Photographs Division
Negative LC–USP6–6531–A

142. *View of west main pavilion stonework*
Photograph, June 13, 1893
Prints and Photographs Division
Negative LC–USZ62–73602

Sculpture

Among the early photographs of the building are views of Bela Lyon Pratt's models for "The Seasons" and of the four bas-reliefs after their installation, as well as a view of Philip Martiny's high reliefs of figures placed beneath the rotunda's interior dome. A few pictures of the statues were made before their installation in the 1890's, and the pictures of the Main Reading Room's symbolic and portrait statues and John Flanagan's sculptures for the clock were taken after the room was renovated in 1964–65.

143. *Sculpted female figures above rotunda, Main Reading Room*
By Philip Martiny
Photograph, ca. 1895
Prints and Photographs Division
Negative LC–USZ62–60738

For further examples of sculpture, see the Slide Show: Decorating the Building, pages 96–99.

Murals

Drawings the artist creates as he develops his preliminary ideas for a painting let the viewer glimpse his evolving thought about his subject. Even when the drawing conforms to the ultimate composition, its freshness and informality hold great charm and give it special value. The Library is fortunate to hold a group of Vedder's sketches for his murals, acquired at various times over the years, and a collection of drawings by Kenyon Cox—the gift of his son Allyn—for the Cox paintings in the large tympanums of the southwest gallery, "The Sciences" and "The Arts."

Many of the Library's murals were photographed on glass-plate negatives around the turn of the century. Even in black and white, these photographs show how the murals looked when they were fresh and new. Other murals have been filmed in recent years in both black and white and color.

144. *"Government"*
Mural by Elihi Vedder
Photograph, ca. 1896–1900
Prints and Photographs Division
Negative LC–USP6–397–C

145. *"Corrupt Legislation"*
Mural by Elihi Vedder
Photograph, ca. 1896–1900
Prints and Photographs Division
Negative LC–USP6–2656–C

146. *Study for mural "Corrupt Legislation"*
By Elihu Vedder
Charcoal and chalk on blue paper, ca. 1895, 51.5 x 39.6 cm
Prints and Photographs Division

147. *Study for mural "Corrupt Legislation"*
By Elihu Vedder
Charcoal and chalk on blue paper, ca. 1895, 55.7 x 39.2 cm
Prints and Photographs Division

148. *"Anarchy"*
Mural by Elihu Vedder
Photograph, ca. 1896–1900
Prints and Photographs Division
Negative LC–USP6–392–C

149. *Study for mural "Anarchy"*
By Elihu Vedder
Pastel on blue paper, ca. 1895, 23.0 x 41.0 cm
Prints and Photographs Division

150. *Study for mural "Anarchy"*
By Elihu Vedder
Charcoal and chalk on brown paper, ca. 1895, 54.8 x 38.0 cm
Prints and Photographs Division

151. *Study for mural "Anarchy"*
By Elihu Vedder
Charcoal and chalk on brown paper, ca. 1895, 47.5 x 31.3 cm
Prints and Photographs Division

152. *Study for the figure "Ignorance" for the mural "Anarchy"*
By Elihu Vedder
Pastel on paper, ca. 1895, 30.5 x 19.4 cm
Prints and Photographs Division

153. *"Good Administration"*
Mural by Elihu Vedder
Photograph, ca. 1896–1900
Prints and Photographs Division
Negative LC–USZ62–73573

154. *Studies for murals "Peace and Prosperity" and "Good Administration"*
By Elihu Vedder
Charcoal and chalk on green paper, ca. 1895, 43.2 x 31.8 cm
Prints and Photographs Division

155. *"Peace and Prosperity"*
Mural by Elihu Vedder
Photograph, ca. 1896–1900
Prints and Photographs Division
Negative LC–USP6–1581–C

156. *Study for mural "Peace and Prosperity"*
By Elihu Vedder
Pastel on blue paper, ca. 1895, 22.3 x 37.2 cm
Prints and Photographs Division

157. *Study for mural "Peace and Prosperity"*
By Elihu Vedder
Charcoal and chalk on blue paper, ca. 1895, 34.2 x 48.3 cm
Prints and Photographs Division

158. *Study for the figure "Agriculture" for the mural "Peace and Prosperity"*
By Elihu Vedder
Charcoal and chalk on green paper, ca. 1895, 32.5 x 26.3 cm
Prints and Photographs Division

159. *"Melpomene"*
Mural by Edward Simmons
Photograph, ca. 1896–1909
Prints and Photographs Division
Negative LC–USP6–396–C

160. *"Clio"*
Mural by Edward Simmons
Photograph, ca. 1909
Prints and Photographs Division
Negative LC–USP6–8651–A

161. *"Thalia"*
Mural by Edward Simmons
Photograph, ca. 1909
Prints and Photographs Division
Negative LC–USP6–8653–A

162. *"Euterpe"*
Mural by Edward Simmons
Photograph, ca. 1900
Prints and Photographs Division
Negative LC–USP6–8652–A

163. *"Terpsichore"*
Mural by Edward Simmons
Photograph, ca. 1909
Prints and Photographs Division
Negative LC–USP6–8649–A

164. *"Erato"*
Mural by Edward Simmons
Photograph from Howard Grey Douglas, THE LIBRARY OF CONGRESS, WASHINGTON, D.C.; ITS PRINCIPAL ARCHITECTURAL AND DECORATIVE FEATURES IN THE COLORS OF THE ORIGINALS (Washington, D.C., 1901)

Photoduplication Service files
Negative LC–USP6–8768–A

165. *"Polyhymnia"*
Mural by Edward Simmons
Photograph, ca. 1909
Prints and Photographs Division
Negative LC–USP6–8650–A

166. *"Urania"*
Mural by Edward Simmons
Photograph, ca. 1899
Prints and Photographs Division
Negative LC–USP6–8648–A

167. *"Calliope"*
Mural by Edward Simmons
Photograph, ca. 1900
Prints and Photographs Division
Negative LC–USP6–394–C

168. *"Paris"*
Mural by Walter McEwen
Photograph, ca. 1909
Prints and Photographs Division
Negative LC–USZ62–17379

169. *"Jason"*
Mural by Walter McEwen
Photograph, ca. 1909
Prints and Photographs Division
Negative LC–USZ62–17378

170. *"Bellerophon"*
Mural by Walter McEwen
Photograph, ca. 1909
Prints and Photographs Division
Negative LC–USZ62–17382

171. *"Orpheus"*
Mural by Walter McEwen
Photograph, ca. 1909
Prints and Photographs Division
Negative LC–USZ62–73551

172. *"Perseus"*
Mural by Walter McEwen
Photograph, ca. 1909
Prints and Photographs Division
Negative LC–USZ62–73572

173. *"Prometheus"*
Mural by Walter McEwen
Photograph, ca. 1909
Prints and Photographs Division
Negative LC–USP6–8723–A

174. *"Theseus"*
Mural by Walter McEwen
Photograph, ca. 1900
Prints and Photographs Division
Negative LC–USZ62–17381

175. *"Achilles"*
Mural by Walter McEwen
Photograph, ca. 1909
Prints and Photographs Division
Negative LC–USZ62–73571

176. *"Hercules"*
Mural by Walter McEwen
Photograph, ca. 1909
Prints and Photographs Division
Negative LC–USZ62–73570

177. *"The Family"*
Mural by Charles Sprague Pearce
Photograph, ca. 1899
Prints and Photographs Division
Negative LC–USP6–400–C

178. *"Religion"*
Mural by Charles Sprague Pearce
Photograph, ca. 1899
Prints and Photographs Division
Negative LC–USP6–399–C

179. *"Labor"*
Mural by Charles Sprague Pearce
Photograph, ca. 1899
Prints and Photographs Division
Negative LC–USZ62–415–B

180. *"Study"*
Mural by Charles Sprague Pearce
Photograph, undated
Prints and Photographs Division
Negative LC–USZ61–417–B

181. *"Rest"*
Mural by Charles Sprague Pearce
Photograph, ca. 1899
Prints and Photographs Division
Negative LC–USZ61–420–B

182. *"Recreation"*
Mural by Charles Sprague Pearce
Photograph, ca. 1899
Prints and Photographs Division
Negative LC–USZ61–416–B

183. *"Instruction"*
Mural by Charles Sprague Pearce
Photograph, ca. 1899
Prints and Photographs Division
Negative LC–USZ62–3202

184. *"Lyric Poetry"*
Mural by Henry Oliver Walker
Photograph, ca. 1898–99
Prints and Photographs Division
Negative LC–USA55–2652–A

185 *"Ganymede"*
Mural by Henry Oliver Walker
Photograph, ca. 1898–99
Prints and Photographs Division
Negative LC–USA55–2649–A

186. *"Endymion"*
Mural by Henry Oliver Walker
Photograph, ca. 1898–99
Prints and Photographs Division
Negative LC–USP6–393–C

187. *"Boy of Winander"*
Mural by Henry Oliver Walker
Photograph, ca. 1898–99
Prints and Photographs Division
Negative LC–USP6–4293–C

188. *"Uriel"*
Mural by Henry Oliver Walker
Photograph, ca. 1898–99
Prints and Photographs Division
Negative LC–USA55–2648–A

189. *"Comus"*
Mural by Henry Oliver Walker
Photograph, ca. 1898–99
Prints and Photographs Division
Negative LC–USZ62–17906

190. *"Adonis"*
Mural by Henry Oliver Walker
Photograph, ca. 1898–99
Prints and Photographs Division
Negative LC–USA55–2651–A

191. *"The Poets"*
Mural by Henry Oliver Walker
Photograph, 1963
Photoduplication Service files
Negative LC–USP6–4308–C

192. *"Fortitude"*
Mural by George Willoughby Maynard
Photograph, ca. 1900
Prints and Photographs Division
Negative LC–USZ62–1008

193. *"Justice"*
Mural by George Willoughby Maynard
Photograph, ca. 1900
Prints and Photographs Division
Negative LC–USP6–6634–A

194. *"Patriotism"*
Mural by George Willoughby Maynard
Photograph, ca. 1900
Prints and Photographs Division
Negative LC–USZ62–1007

195. *"Courage"*
Mural by George Willoughby Maynard
Photograph, ca. 1900
Prints and Photographs Division
Negative LC–USZ62–1010

196. *"Temperance"*
Mural by George Willoughby Maynard
Photograph, ca. 1899
Prints and Photographs Division
Negative LC–USP6–6637–A

197. *"Prudence"*
Mural by George Willoughby Maynard
Photograph, ca. 1899
Prints and Photographs Division
Negative LC–USZ62–1009

198. *"Industry"*
Mural by George Willoughby Mayard
Photograph, ca. 1900
Prints and Photographs Division
Negative LC–USP6–6635–A

199. *"Concordia"*
Mural by George Willoughby Maynard
Photograph, ca. 1900

Prints and Photographs Division
Negative LC–USP6–6636–A

200. *"Lyrica"*
Mural by George Randolph Barse, Jr.
Photograph, undated
Prints and Photographs Division
Negative LC–USP6–8271–M–4

201. *"Tragedy"*
Mural by George Randolph Barse, Jr.
Photograph, undated
Prints and Photographs Division
Negative LC–USP6–8271–M–9

202. *"Comedy"*
Mural by George Randolph Barse, Jr.
Photograph, undated
Prints and Photographs Division
Negative LC–USP6–8271–M–13

203. *"History"*
Mural by George Randolph Barse, Jr.
Photograph, undated
Prints and Photographs Division
Negative LC–USP6–8271–M–19

204. *"Erotica"*
Mural by George Randolph Barse, Jr.
Photograph, undated
Prints and Photographs Division
Negative LC–USP6–8272–M–35

205. *"Tradition"*
Mural by George Randolph Barse, Jr.
Photograph, undated
Prints and Photographs Division
Negative LC–USP6–8273–M–21A

206. *"Fancy"*
Mural by George Randolph Barse, Jr.
Photograph, undated
Prints and Photographs Division
Negative LC–USP6–8272–M–26

207. *"Romance"*
Mural by George Randolph Barse, Jr.
Photograph, undated
Prints and Photographs Division
Negative LC–USP6–8272–M–23

208. *"Zoology"*
Mural by Walter Shirlaw
Photograph, ca. 1898
Prints and Photographs Division
Negative LC–USP6–8726

209. *"Physics"*
Mural by Walter Shirlaw
Photograph, ca. 1898
Prints and Photographs Division
Negative LC–USP6–8725

210. *"Geology"*
Mural by Walter Shirlaw
Photograph, ca. 1898
Prints and Photographs Division
Negative LC–USP6–8730

211. *"Mathematics"*
Mural by Walter Shirlaw
Photograph, ca. 1898
Prints and Photographs Division
Negative LC–USP6–8727

212. *"Archaeology"*
Mural by Walter Shirlaw
Photograph, ca. 1898
Prints and Photographs Division
Negative LC–USP6–8722

213. *"Botany"*
Mural by Walter Shirlaw
Photograph, ca. 1898
Prints and Photographs Division
Negative LC–USP6–8728

214. *"Astronomy"*
Mural by Walter Shirlaw
Photograph, ca. 1898
Prints and Photographs Division
Negative LC–USP6–8724

215. *"Chemistry"*
Mural by Walter Shirlaw
Photograph, ca. 1898
Prints and Photographs Division
Negative LC–USP6–8729

216. *"War"*
Mural by Julius Gari Melchers
Photograph, ca. 1909
Prints and Photographs Division
Negative LC–USP6–5436–A

217. *"Peace"*
Mural by Julius Gari Melchers
Photograph, ca. 1909
Prints and Photographs Division
Negative LC–USP6–5437–A

218. *"The Arts"*
Mural by Kenyon Cox
Photograph, 1896
Prints and Photographs Division
Negative LC–USP6–1688–A

219. *Oil study for mural "The Arts"*
By Kenyon Cox
Oil on canvas, ca. 1895, 40.6 x 99.4 cm
Prints and Photographs Division

220. *Study of the nude figure "Music" for mural "The Arts"*
By Kenyon Cox
Pencil on paper, ca. 1895, 51.4 x 40.7 cm
Prints and Photographs Division

221. *Study of draped figure "Music" for mural "The Arts"*
By Kenyon Cox
Pencil on paper, ca. 1895, 51.5 x 36.4 cm
Prints and Photographs Division

222. *"The Sciences"*
Mural by Kenyon Cox
Photograph, 1896
Prints and Photographs Division
Negative LC–USP6–1688–A

223. *Oil study for mural "The Sciences"*
By Kenyon Cox
Oil on canvas, ca. 1895–96, 38.5 x 99.5 cm
Prints and Photographs Division

224. *Oil study of peacock for mural "The Sciences"*
By Kenyon Cox
Oil on canvas, ca. 1895–96, 80.7 x 60.3 cm
Prints and Photographs Division

225. *Study of nude figure of "Physics" for mural "The Sciences"*
By Kenyon Cox
Pencil on paper, ca. 1895–96, 50.8 x 39.8 cm
Prints and Photographs Division

226. *Study of draped figure "Physics" for mural "The Sciences"*
By Kenyon Cox
Pencil on paper, ca. 1895–96, 51.5 x 38.0 cm
Prints and Photographs Division

227. *Study of the figure "Genius with Telescope" for mural "The Sciences"*
By Kenyon Cox
Pencil on paper, ca. 1895–96, 50.9 x 39.8 cm
Prints and Photographs Division

228. *The Departments of the Treasury and of State*
Mural by William Brantley Van Ingen
Photograph, 1972
Photoduplication Service files
Negative LC–USP6–6584–C

229. *The Departments of Agriculture and of the Interior*
Mural by William Brantley Van Ingen
Photograph, 1972
Photoduplication Service files
Negative LC–USP6–6582–C

230. *The Departments of Justice and of the Post Office*
Mural by William Brantley Van Ingen
Photograph, 1972
Photoduplication Service files
Negative LC–USP6–6581–C

231. *The Departments of War and of the Navy*
Mural by William Brantley Van Ingen
Photograph, 1972
Photoduplication Service files
Negative LC–USP6–6583–C

232. *"Science"*
Mural by William de Leftwich Dodge
Photograph, 1976
Photoduplication Service files
Negative LC–USP6–7246–C

233. *"Music"*
Mural by William de Leftwich Dodge
Photograph, 1976
Photoduplication Service files
Negative LC–USP6–7242–C

234. *"Art"*
Mural by William de Leftwich Dodge
Photograph, 1976
Photoduplication Service files
Negative LC–USP6–7243–C

80

235. *"Literature"*
Mural by William de Leftwich Dodge
Photograph, 1976
Photoduplication Service files
Negative LC–USP6–7245–C

236. *"Earth"*
Mural by Robert L. Dodge
Photograph by Wilbur L. Wright, ca. 1899
Prints and Photographs Division
Negative LC–USP6–6717–A

237. *"Fire"*
Mural by Robert L. Dodge
Photograph by Wilbur L. Wright, ca. 1899
Prints and Photographs Division
Negative LC–USP6–6715–A

238. *"Water"*
Mural by Robert L. Dodge
Photograph by Wilbur L. Wright, ca. 1899
Prints and Photographs Division
Negative LC–USP6–6716–A

239. *"Air"*
Mural by Robert L. Dodge
Photograph by Wilbur L. Wright, ca. 1899
Prints and Photographs Division
Negative LC–USP6–6718–A

240. *"Adventure"*
Mural by George Willoughby Maynard
Photograph, ca. 1898
Prints and Photographs Division
Negative LC–USP6–6640–A

241. *"Discovery"*
Mural by George Willoughby Maynard
Photograph, ca. 1898
Prints and Photographs Division
Negative LC–USP6–6638–A

242. *"Conquest"*
Mural by George Willoughby Maynard
Photograph, ca. 1898
Prints and Photographs Division
Negative LC–USP6–6639–A

243. *"Civilization"*
Mural by George Willoughby Maynard
Photograph, ca. 1898
Prints and Photographs Division
Negative LC–USZ62–73567

For further examples of murals, see the Slide Show: Decorating the Building, pages 96-99.

Mosaics

For the vaulted ceilings of marble mosaic in the north, south, and east galleries adjoining the staircase hall of the Great Hall, Herman T. Schladermundt prepared the working cartoons after preliminary sketches by Edward Pearce Casey. Emblems of the various arts and sciences and the names of famous men in those fields appear in these three galleries. In areas of the second floor, mosaics are also used in the floors themselves.

For Elihu Vedder's mosaic of "The Minerva of Peace," created in Italy, the Library has the artist's pastel study. Early photographs of the 1890's record Frederick Dielman's mosaics of "Law" and "History," also executed in Italy, as well as his sketch for the latter mosaic.

244. *Study for mosaic "The Minerva of Peace"*
By Elihu Vedder
Pastel on gray paper, ca. 1896, 53.3 x 36.0 cm
Prints and Photographs Division

245. *"The Minerva of Peace"*
Mosaic by Elihu Vedder
Photograph, May 4, 1964
Photoduplication Service files

246. *View of mosaics in vaulted ceilings, east side, Great Hall, leading to the Main Reading Room*
Designed by Edward Pearce Casey
Photograph, ca. 1945
Photoduplication Service files
Negative LC–USP6–126–A

247. *View of mosaics in vaulted ceilings, east side, Great Hall*
Designed by Edward Pearce Casey
Photograph, ca. 1945
Photoduplication Service files
Negative LC–USP6–2–A

248. *"Law"*
Detail of mosaic by Frederick Dielman
Photograph by Wilbur L. Wright, ca. 1899
Prints and Photographs Division
Negative LC–USZ62–73603

249. *"Law"*
Mosaic by Frederick Dielman
Photograph, ca. 1895
Prints and Photographs Division
Negative LC–USP6–401–C

250. *Study for the mosaic "History"*
By Frederick Dielman
Photograph, ca. 1900
Prints and Photographs Division
Negative LC–USZ62–22325

For further examples of mosaics, see the Slide Show: Decorating the Building, pages 96-99.

Furnishing the Building: 1897-1903

More than construction and decoration was required to complete the Library of Congress building. It also had to be furnished. Although basic furnishings were installed before it opened in November 1897, much remained to be done as funds permitted and as time in the new quarters revealed new needs.

In his annual report for the fiscal year that ended June 30, 1898, Superintendent Green noted that furniture for the principal reading rooms and offices had been installed, that the "general fitting up" of the Copyright Office had been accomplished, and that "part of the permanent cases for the exhibition halls" were in place.

Funds for the next fiscal year secured display cases in 1898 for the west exhibition halls and special safe cases for manuscripts. Still in the planning stage in 1898 were furnishings for the areas housing the newspapers and periodicals, music, and maps. Of these collections, Green wrote: "Steps . . . are being taken slowly and cautiously to insure . . . the best permanent results under the new conditions peculiar to their proper establishment in the new building."

Apart from the special designs required for housing the collections and serving readers, the design of the building itself sometimes dictated the design of the furniture. The rotunda, for example, demanded a circular service desk, a curving card catalog, and curved desks for readers. The responsibility for designing such custom-built furniture fell to architect Casey.

Among the drawings for details of the brickwork, ironwork, stonework, copperwork, tiles, and mosaics are drawings for all types of office and library furniture. The drawings are sometimes initialed by the draftsman but stamped with the seal of Casey's New York office.

The results were sturdy, attractive furnishings that blended with the building's style. The work equipment was designed to be useful, and the readers' chairs were comfortable.

More original furniture remains in use today than might be expected. Comfortable settees of light oak, designed for visitors touring the building and used by at least five generations, remain a familiar sight in the halls today. Although the readers' chairs in the Main Reading Room had to be replaced after more than half a century of hard use, the central desk and readers' desks were simply refinished. A number of oak reading or writing tables from other reading rooms continue to be used in workplaces. Some of them have been refinished. Original chairs from the early House and Senate Reading Rooms and from the Main Reading Room are included in the exhibition. Lighting fixtures from the Main Reading Room and the office of the Librarian of Congress are also among the furnishings displayed.

One drawing depicts the long rectangular table of oak designed for the Senate Reading Room and the oak desk for the Librarian. Bearing the initials "R. K. S." and the seal of Casey's office, the drawing is dated May 1, 1897. The design for the Senators' table shows clearly the carved griffins on the legs.

The Librarian's desk has proved as durable as it is handsome. It has served six Librarians of Congress: John Russell Young (1897–99),

Herbert Putnam (1899–1939), Archibald MacLeish (1939–44), Luther Harris Evans (1945–53), Lawrence Quincy Mumford (1954–74), and Daniel J. Boorstin, the present Librarian of Congress.

251. *"View of Interior of Book Stack in Any Tier"*
Designed by Bernard Richardson Green
Photograph of ink drawing, ca. 1895
Photoduplication Service files
Negative LC–USP6–6506–A

252. *"Furniture for Building for Library of Congress"*
Designed by Edward Pearce Casey, May 1, 1897
Photograph of ink drawing, 54.0 x 68.5 cm
Library of Congress Archives, Central Services Division
Negative LC–USZ6–1088

253. *"Library Furniture"*
Design attributed to Edward Pearce Casey
Photograph of ink drawing, 56.0 x 87.5 cm
Library of Congress Archives, Central Services Division
Negative LC–USZ6–1089

254. *"Library of Congress. Reader's Chair"*
Designed by Edward Pearce Casey
Photograph, undated
Prints and Photographs Division
Negative LC–USP6–6612–A

255. *"Full Size Detail of Reading Table"*
Design attributed to Edward Pearce Casey
Photograph of ink drawing, December 2, 1903, 83.1 x 69.8 cm
Library of Congress Archives, Central Services Division
Negative LC–USZ6–1090

256. *"Furniture for Building for Library of Congress"*
Designed by Edward Pearce Casey, May 1, 1897
Photograph of ink drawing, 79.5 x 63.5 cm
Library of Congress Archives, Central Services Division
Negative LC–USZ6–1091

257. *"6 Lt. Elec. Chand[elier]"*
Photograph of ink drawing, 42.1 x 30.4 cm
Library of Congress Archives, Central Services Division
Negative LC–USZ6–1092

258. *Lighting Fixtures*
Photograph, ca. 1897
Prints and Photographs Division
Negative LC–USP6–6613–A

259. *Woodwork. Full Size Details of Reading Desks, [Main] Reading Room"*
Photograph of ink drawing, 75.0 x 103.5 cm
Library of Congress Archives, Central Services Division
Negative LC–USZ6–1093

260. *"Woodwork, Centre Desk. Octagon, First Story"*
Photograph of ink drawing, 71.5 x 103.5 cm
Library of Congress Archives, Central Services Division
Negative LC–USZ6–1094

261. *Lamp, originally used in the Main Reading Room*
Buildings Management Division

262. *Lighting fixture, originally used in the Librarian's office*
Bronze
Buildings Management Division

263. *Reading table, originally used in House Reading Room*
Oak
Buildings Management Division

264. *Desk chairs, originally used in House Reading Room*
Oak
Buildings Management Division

265. *Reader's chair, originally used in the Main Reading Room*
Oak
Buildings Management Division

266. *Bench, designed for exhibition halls*
Oak
Buildings Management Division

267. *Desk chair with arms, originally used in Senate Reading Room*
Oak
Buildings Management Division

Instant Tourist Attraction: 1898

Art critics and photographers combined forces with the press throughout the country to publicize "the new Library of Congress," as it was called for several years after the building was opened on November 1, 1897. They tempted more than half a million visitors to its breathtaking premises in the first 11 months of 1898.

Called "Our National Monument of Art" by critic Royal Cortissoz in *Harper's Weekly* (December 28, 1895), the new building literally sparkled inside and out in 1898. In its vast interior spaces, the marbles, mosaics, murals, and sculptures were new and clean and bright then. The halls and galleries were delightfully open, uncluttered, and welcoming. There the Library's fine prints and rare maps and books could be displayed for the public. But the building was an art exhibition in itself.

How it looked to the visitors who gasped at its beauty in 1898 was captured for the 1980's in the remarkable images created by the photographers of that day. The pictures by photographers of the early 20th century are also compelling.

268. *View of Great Hall, west main pavilion*
Photograph from MONOGRAPHS OF AMERICAN ARCHITECTURE, vol. 6 (Boston, Ticknor, 1898)
Prints and Photographs Division
Negative LC–USZ62–47255

269. *View of staircase leading to Visitors' Gallery above Great Hall*
Photograph from MONOGRAPHS OF AMERICAN ARCHITECTURE, vol. 6 (Boston, Ticknor, 1898)
Prints and Photographs Division
Negative LC–USZ62–47261

270. *View of east gallery, second floor, west main pavilion*
Photograph from MONOGRAPHS OF AMERICAN ARCHITECTURE, vol. 6 (Boston, Ticknor, 1898)
Prints and Photographs Division
Negative LC–USZ62–47258

271. *View of southeast pavilion, called the "Pavilion of the Elements"*
Photograph from MONOGRAPHS OF AMERICAN ARCHITECTURE, vol. 6 (Boston, Ticknor, 1898)
Prints and Photographs Division
Negative LC–USZ62–47263

272. *View of south curtain, second floor*
Photograph, ca. 1900
Prints and Photographs Division
Negative LC–USZ62–73604

273. *View of west foyer leading to Great Hall*
Photograph from MONOGRAPHS OF AMERICAN ARCHITECTURE, vol. 6 (Boston, Ticknor, 1898)
Prints and Photographs Division
Negative LC–USZ62–47270

274. *View of sculpted marble arches in Great Hall, west main pavilion*
Photograph from MONOGRAPHS OF AMERICAN ARCHITECTURE, vol. 6 (Boston, Ticknor, 1898)
Prints and Photographs Division
Negative LC–USZ62–47254

275. *View of north gallery, Great Hall*
Photograph from MONOGRAPHS OF AMERICAN ARCHITECTURE, vol. 6 (Boston, Ticknor, 1898)
Prints and Photographs Division
Negative LC–USZ62–47257

276. *View of southwest corridor leading from Great Hall to House and Senate Reading Rooms*
Photograph from MONOGRAPHS OF AMERICAN ARCHITECTURE, vol. 6 (Boston, Ticknor, 1898)
Prints and Photographs Division
Negative LC–USZ62–47269

277. *Carved oak bas-relief above doorway in House Reading Room*
By Charles Henry Niehaus
Photograph from MONOGRAPHS OF AMERICAN ARCHITECTURE, vol. 6 (Boston, Ticknor, 1898)
Prints and Photographs Division
Negative LC–USZ62–47264

278. *View of House of Representatives Reading Room*
Photograph from MONOGRAPHS OF AMERICAN ARCHITECTURE, vol. 6 (Boston, Ticknor, 1898)
Prints and Photographs Division
Negative LC–USZ62–47265

279. *View of Senate Reading Room*
Photograph from MONOGRAPHS OF AMERICAN ARCHITECTURE, vol. 6 (Boston, Ticknor, 1898)
Prints and Photographs Division
Negative LC–USZ62–47271

Souvenirs and Memorabilia

The "most beautiful building I have ever seen," wrote one tourist in her diary in 1908, after visiting the new Library of Congress building. In general, the American people fell in love with it. The building excited the national imagination and national pride, and because it represented a house of learning, the public attached great importance to it.

Entrepreneurs joined in this general excitement. The variety of souvenirs produced for sale to the tourists then and collected now by browsers in secondhand stores is surprising. Souvenir plates, depicting the building as seen from the Capitol and manufactured in England or on the continent, appear to have been especially popular. But the Library's image found its way onto all kinds of objects. Some were charming, some were kitsch; but all sold in the marketplace.

As for memorabilia, families kept diaries and letters and snapshots of their visits. The Library, too, has its own memorabilia, in the great collection of architectural photographs and in its early pictures of the custodial divisions for the collections. There are objects, also—notably "the keys to the Library of Congress." Those displayed are but two of many. Large and heavy—nearly 6 inches in length—one opens the great bronze door at the center of the west main pavilion's main entrance, and the other opens the two bronze doors flanking it. The sculpted doors can be opened only from the interior, however. There are no keyholes in the exteriors of the three bronze doors.

286. *Souvenir plate depicting the Library of Congress*
Inscribed: Wedgwood, Etruria, England

Blue decal on white earthenware, © 1900
Diameter: 24.0 cm
Lent by Mr. and Mrs. Edgar A. Glick, Reston, Virginia

287. *Souvenir plate depicting the Library of Congress*
Inscribed: Silesia
Full-color image on white porcelain, banded in green and gold; undated
Diameter: 19.0 cm
Gift of Grace L. Smiley, St. Louis, Missouri
Information Office

288. *Souvenir plate depicting the Library of Congress*
Inscribed: Frank Beardmore & Co., Fenton
Blue decal on white earthenware, undated
Diameter: 20.0 cm
Gift of Mrs. Douglas A. King, Corona, California
Information Office

289. *Souvenir plate depicting the Library of Congress*
Inscribed: Victoria, Austria
Black decal on a colored ground, banded in coral and blue with patriotic symbols
Diameter: 23.6 cm
Lent by Eugene V. Muench, Terre Haute, Indiana

290. *Souvenir pitcher depicting the Library of Congress and the U. S. Capitol*
Transparent brown glaze over black decal on white earthenware, banded in silver with silver handle
Height: 12.0 cm; base diameter: 6.3 cm
Lent by Mr. and Mrs. William R. Nugent, Reston, Virginia

291. *Souvenir cream-and-sugar tray depicting the Library of Congress*
Inscribed: Made in Germany
Black decal circled in gold on white porcelain, banded in gold with blue fish-scale border, undated
Size: 17.0 x 9.0 x 1.6 cm
Lent by Mr. and Mrs. William R. Nugent, Reston, Virginia

292. *Souvenir plate depicting the Library of Congress in low relief*
Bisque, hand-painted in ecru, green, and gold; undated
Diameter: 26.0 cm
Lent by Mr. and Mrs. Warren R. Johnston, Garrett Park, Maryland

293. *Souvenir bowl depicting tourist attractions of Washington, D.C., including the Library of Congress*
Multicolored images on white porcelain, banded in gold; undated
Diameter: 18.5 cm
Lent by Mr. and Mrs. Warren R. Johnston, Garrett Park, Maryland

294. *Souvenir plate depicting the Library of Congress*
Inscribed: England
Blue decal on white earthenware, undated
Diameter: 23.5 cm
Lent by Mr. and Mrs. Warren R. Johnston, Garrett Park, Maryland

295. *Souvenir plate depicting tourist attractions of Washington, D.C., including the Library of Congress*
Inscribed: England
Blue decal on white earthenware, undated
Diameter: 23.5 cm
Lent by Mr. and Mrs. Warren R. Johnston, Garrett Park, Maryland

296. *Souvenir plate depicting tourist attractions of Washington, D.C., including the Library of Congress*
Inscribed: England
Blue decal on white earthenware, undated
Diameter: 23.0 cm
Lent by Mr. and Mrs. Warren R. Johnston, Garrett Park, Maryland

297. *Souvenir plate depicting the Library of Congress*
Inscribed: Royal Doulton, England
Blue decal on white earthenware, undated
Diameter: 25.5 cm
Lent by Mr. and Mrs. Warren R. Johnston, Garrett Park, Maryland

298. *Souvenir plate depicting the Library of Congress*
Inscribed: England
Cobalt blue on white earthenware, undated
Diameter: 26.0 cm
Lent by Mr. and Mrs. Warren R. Johnston, Garrett Park, Maryland

299. *Heart-shaped souvenir jewelry box depicting tourist attractions of Washington, D.C., including the Library of Congress*
Inscribed: J. B., 2348
Low relief, gold-colored metal, lined; undated
Height: 2.03 cm; width: 6.5 cm
Lent by Mr. and Mrs. Warren R. Johnston, Garrett Park, Maryland

300. *Souvenir tumbler depicting tourist attractions of Washington, D.C., including the Library of Congress*
Inscribed: Made in Germany
Multicolored images on white porcelain, banded in gold; undated

Height: 9.53 cm; diameter: 7.0 cm
Lent by Mr. and Mrs. Warren R. Johnston, Garrett Park, Maryland

301. *Souvenir glass paperweight depicting the Library of Congress*
Colored image detailed with gold foil, undated
Size: 1.5 x 10.5 x 6.5 cm
Lent by Mr. and Mrs. Warren R. Johnston, Garrett Park, Maryland

302. *Souvenir snuffbox or pillbox depicting the Library of Congress*
Low relief, silver-colored metal with flowered art nouveau design; undated
Height: 2.0 cm; diameter: 4.0 cm
Gift of Mr. and Mrs. Eldon Marcum, Cincinnati, Ohio
Information Office

303. *Souvenir spoon depicting in its ladle the Library of Congress*
Silver, low relief; undated
Length: 14.3 cm
Lent by Mrs. Corinne Friedman, San Francisco, California, and Washington, D.C.

304. *Keys for the Library of Congress main entrance*
Special Police Office

305. *Diary entry, September 24, 1908, of visit to the Library of Congress*
By Mrs. Arthur C. McCain, Augusta, Montana
Manuscript
Lent by Jon D. Freshour, Washington, D.C.

306. THE LIBRARY OF CONGRESS, WASHINGTON, D.C.; ITS PRINCIPAL ARCHITECTURAL AND DECORATIVE FEATURES IN THE COLORS OF THE ORIGINALS (*Washington, D.C., 1901*)
By Howard Grey Douglas
Information Office

307. *Souvenir plate depicting the Library of Congress*
Inscribed: Frank Beardmore & Co., Fenton, England
Transparent brown glaze over black decal on white earthenware, undated
Diameter: 23.4 cm
Lent by Mr. and Mrs. Edgar A. Glick, Reston, Virginia

308. *Souvenir plate depicting the Library of Congress*
Inscribed: Johnson Bros., England
Multicolored image on white earthenware, banded in gold; undated
Diameter: 18.4 cm
Lent by Mr. and Mrs. Edgar A. Glick, Reston, Virginia

309. *Souvenir plate depicting the Library of Congress*
Inscribed: Silesia
Multicolored image on white porcelain, banded in gold
Diameter: 17.2 cm
Lent by Mr. and Mrs. Edgar A. Glick, Reston, Virginia

310. *Powder jar depicting the Library of Congress*
Inscribed: Germany
Lid: Black decal on white porcelain, bordered in cobalt blue
Footed dish: Pink and green floral garland beneath cobalt blue border on white porcelain, banded in gold
Height: 5.1 cm; diameter: 8.9 cm
Lent by Mr. and Mrs. Edgar A. Glick, Reston, Virginia

311. *School children at Neptune Fountain*
Photograph by Frances Benjamin Johnston, ca. 1899
Prints and Photographs Division
Negative LC–USZ62–4546

312. *Visitors posing at Neptune Fountain*
Photograph by Underwood & Underwood, ca. 1920
Prints and Photographs Division
Negative LC–USZ62–73569

313. *"American Fashions," depicting Great Hall of Library of Congress in background*
Published by Jno. J. Mitchell Co., New York, August 1899
Colored lithograph, 56.5 x 70.9 cm
Prints and Photographs Division

New Construction, New Contours

Five construction projects in the 20th century changed the contours of the 1897 building. With the spurt in publishing in this country and abroad early in the century, the collections required more space—space which the building's original design allowed. A new bookstack filled the southeast courtyard in 1910, and another was built in the northeast courtyard in 1926.

The need for a proper home for the Library's growing collection of rare books, where they could be protected by controlled temperature and humidity, was met in 1930–35 by the construction of a pavilion at the center of the building's east front. Beneath the Rare Book Room and its bookstacks on the second floor, the pavilion gave space on the main floor to the catalog cards of the National Union Catalog, begun in 1901, adjacent to the Main Reading Room's card catalog.

Two construction projects were the gifts of private donors to enliven the Library's music collections with public activities. Elizabeth Sprague Coolidge donated the funds to build an auditorium for chamber music concerts in the northwest courtyard in 1925. To the courtyard grounds in 1928, she added a small reflecting pool. Gertrude Clarke Whittall, who gave the Library a magnificent set of five Stradivarius instruments and five Tourte bows in 1936 for performance in concerts, donated funds to construct the Whittall Pavilion. Adjoining the Coolidge Auditorium, it houses the instruments between concerts and provides a setting for related cultural events. In the niche of the retaining wall of the steps leading from the pavilion to the reflecting pool, she placed Frederick Macmonnies' bronze statue "Pan of Rohallion."

314. *Constructing bookstack in northeast courtyard*
Photograph, June 23, 1926
Prints and Photographs Division
Negative LC–USZ62–57608

315. *Artist's sketch for east front extension*
Photograph by Abel & Company Commercial Photographers, Washington, D.C., undated
Information Office files
Negative LC–USZ62–73605

316. *Aerial view showing construction of the east front extension*
Photograph, 1933
Prints and Photographs Division
Negative LC–USZ62–73534

317. *Bronze doors of Rare Book Room*
Photograph, ca. 1949
Photoduplication Service files
Negative LC–USP6–466–A

318. *View of Rare Book Room*
Photograph, ca. 1949
Photoduplication Service files
Negative LC–USP6–1476–A

319. *Elizabeth Sprague Coolidge (1864–1953)*
Photograph of a 1923 portrait by John Singer Sargent
Photoduplication Service files
Negative LC–SP6–466–A

320. *Interior view from the stage of Coolidge Auditorium during a concert of the Budapest String Quartet*
Photograph, April 7, 1960
Photoduplication Service files
Negative LC–USP6–3754–A

321. *Interior view from the entrance of Coolidge Auditorium during a Juilliard String Quartet concert*
Photograph, undated
Photoduplication Service files
Negative LC–USP6–8307–M–24

322. *Gertrude Clarke Whittall (1867–1965)*
Photograph, undated
Music Division

323. *Wrought iron doors, Whittall Pavilion*
Photograph, undated
Photoduplication Service files
Negative LC–USP6–8293–M–20

324. *Interior of Whittall Pavilion*
  Photograph, undated
  Photoduplication Service files
  Negative LC–USP6–3884–A

325. *View of northwest courtyard outside Whittall Pavilion*
  Photograph, early 1940's
  Photoduplication Service files
  Negative LC–USP6–81–A

Renovation

Maintaining a vast and heavily used public building is a continuing job that challenges the imagination. During the 1960's, several operations of magnitude were undertaken to clean, renovate, and restore areas of the 1897 building by the Architect of the Capitol in cooperation with the Library. One project was the installation of a new heating and ventilation system for the entire building, in which air conditioning had been limited to the Rare Book Room of 1935. Staff members and the Library's users, who had suffered the heat and humidity of Washington's summers for many years, were amused to learn that they were merely the secondary beneficiaries of the new air conditioning. Its primary purpose was to protect the Library's books and other collections.

The renovating projects disrupted operations of the Library staff as workmen moved from area to area. But when they were done, the stonework of the exterior granite could be appreciated for its beauty and workmanship again, the bronze statues of the Main Reading Room were again the color of bronze, and, when the Main Reading Room was cleaned, the gold mosaic that John Flanagan had designed for the background of his "Father Time" was rediscovered.

326. *Bronze doors, main entrance, before cleaning*
Photograph, October 29, 1946
Photoduplication Service files
Negative LC–USP6–157–A

327. *Bronze doors, main entrance, after cleaning*
Photograph, July 1961
Photoduplication Service files
Negative LC–USP6–4052–A

328. *Steam cleaning, west facade*
Photograph, February 5, 1962
Photoduplication Service files
Negative LC–USP6–4126–C

329. *Steam cleaning, west facade*
Photograph, 1962
Photoduplication Service files
Negative LC–USP6–4122–C

330. *View of pillars, Great Hall, showing cleaning in progress*
Photograph, November 4, 1964
Photoduplication Service files
Negative LC–USP6–4550–C

331. *View of Coolidge Auditorium during renovation*
Photograph, August 1962
Photoduplication Service files
Negative LC–USP6–4295–A

332. *Renovation, Coolidge Auditorium*
Photograph, 1962
Photoduplication Service files
Negative LC–USP6–3916–C

333. *View of scaffolding in Main Reading Room during renovation*
Photograph, November 20, 1964
Photoduplication Service files
Negative LC–USP6–4553–C

334. *View of scaffolding and dome, Main Reading Room, during renovation*
Black-and-white slide, January 5, 1965
Photoduplication Service files
Negative LC–USP6–4558–C

335. *View of dome, Main Reading Room, after renovation*
Color slide, 1980
Prints and Photographs Division
Negative LC–USZ62–73559 (black-and-white)

336. *Fish-eye view of rotunda and dome, Main Reading Room, after renovation*
Photograph, 1966
Photoduplication Service files
Negative LC–USP6–4730–M

337. *View of dome, Main Reading Room, during renovation*
Photograph, June 1965
Photoduplication Service files
Negative LC–USP6–4753–C

338. *Sculpture of "Herodotus," Main Reading Room, flanked by scaffolding during renovation*
Photograph, 1965
Office of the Architect of the Capitol
Negative 27674

339. *Sculpture of "Philosophy" before cleaning and restoration*
Photograph, 1965
Office of the Architect of the Capitol
Negative 27675

340. *Vacuuming the dome during renovation*
Photograph, 1965
Office of the Architect of the Capitol
Negative 27531

341. *Detail of dome before cleaning*
Photograph, 1965

Office of the Architect of the Capitol
Negative 27528

342. *Detail of dome during restoration*
Photograph, 1965
Office of the Architect of the Capitol
Negative 27527

343. *Bronze sculpture of "Father Time" and "The Seasons" after cleaning*
By John F. Flanagan
Photograph, 1965
Office of the Architect of the Capitol
Negative 27681

Space Problems: 1955-80

While the building was undergoing renovation in the 1960's, its cellar and storage spaces were being converted to workspaces, as were like spaces in the 1939 annex (now the John Adams Building). Overcrowding led to drastic solutions. When the bookstacks could absorb no more extra shelving, books were double-shelved, then stacked on floors. And when no more staff could be divorced from the collections by moves to rental quarters, the public galleries gave way to desks and shelves and filing cabinets. While the Library awaited its third building, it was 1872-to-1897 revisited.

By the late 1960's, the public exhibition halls were disfigured by partitions. These allowed for lighting for work areas and heat against the winter chill of marble floors beneath the soaring, vaulted ceilings. In the end, partitions invaded three-quarters of the Great Hall's upper level, creeping around Corinthian columns and hiding murals and sculpture.

In the Main Reading Room, seven sides of the octagonal Visitors' Gallery were closed. But there the partitions did not—indeed, could not—obscure the bronze portrait statues, so newly refurbished in 1965. Shakespeare, Homer, Bacon, Plato, and all the others, mounted as they are on the gallery's marble railing, forced the partitions to duck around them in a strange zigzag pattern.

Visitors mourned their visual loss. Staff members forced into galleries, staff members exiled from the collections, and staff members who had known the beauty of "the old building" grieved even more. The Library's plans eventually to restore the building gave little comfort. Only the 1971 groundbreaking for the third building offered hope.

But with the spring of 1980, hope became reality. The Geography and Map Division, with its rare records of the earth's globe, was recalled to Capitol Hill from 12 miles away in Virginia to occupy its new quarters in the Library of Congress James Madison Memorial Building. Day by day, Congressional Research Service staff packed their files in the galleries above the Library's Great Hall, preparing to leave there for their offices across the street. At last the Visitors' Gallery above the Main Reading Room, the southwest gallery and its pavilion, and the hidden areas of the Great Hall's second floor were finally emptied.

As the heat wave of Washington's summer began, the ugly partitions were torn away from the marble. The years have taken their toll, but staff members who had never before seen the great galleries gasped, as had the tourists of an earlier day. And staff members who remembered the galleries of the 1950's marveled, for they had forgotten how vast and how impressive they were.

344. *View of overcrowded bookstack*
Photograph, January 30, 1970
Photoduplication Service files
Negative LC–USP6–5813–C

345. *View of overcrowded bookstack*
Photograph, May 2, 1971
Photoduplication Service files
Negative LC–USP6–6198–C

346. *View of partitions and crowded workspace, Visitors' Gallery, Main Reading Room*
Photograph, February 13, 1969
Photoduplication Service files
Negative LC–USP6–5479–C

347. *View of partitions and crowded workspace, Visitors' Gallery, Main Reading Room*
Photograph, February 13, 1969

Photoduplication Service files
Negative LC–USP6–5478–C

348. *View of office partitions, Great Hall exhibition galleries*
Photograph, February 13, 1969
Photoduplication Service files
Negative LC–USP6–5487–C

349. *View of office partitions, Great Hall exhibition galleries*
Photograph, February 13, 1969

Photoduplication Service files
Negative LC–USP6–5475–C

350. *Office workspace, Great Hall exhibition galleries*
Photograph, February 13, 1969
Photoduplication Service files
Negative LC–USP6–5483–C

351. *Office partitions, Great Hall exhibition galleries*
Photograph, February 19, 1969
Photoduplication Service files
Negative LC–USP6–5485–C

Slide Show: Constructing the Building

S1. *Site of the Library's future building as seen from the Capitol, looking east down East Capitol Street*
See item 41

S2. *Site of the Library's future building as seen from the Capitol looking southeast, with Pennsylvania Avenue on the right*
See item 42

S3. *View of the excavation for the Library of Congress building*
See item 43

S4. *Foundation work in progress*
Photograph, 1889
Prints and Photographs Division
Negative LC–USZ62–51457

S5. *View of excavation for the Library of Congress building*
Photograph, September 12, 1888
Prints and Photographs Division
LC–USP6–6508–A

S6. *Brickmasons at work on the foundation*
See item 60

S7. *View of foundation, looking toward Capitol*
See item 57

S8. *Laying the cornerstone of the northwest pavilion*
See item 59

S9. *View of foundation rising*
Photograph, 1889
Prints and Photographs Division
Negative LC–USZ62–73562

S10. *View of the basement level, looking toward the Capitol*
Photograph, October 3, 1890
Prints and Photographs Division
LC–USZ62–73563

S11. *Laying the cornerstone of the Northeast Pavilion*
See item 63

S12. *View of construction showing four levels at different stages of completion*
Photograph, July 10, 1891
Prints and Photographs Division
Negative LC–USZ62–73564

S13. *View of the brick arches in the basement of the west main pavilion, looking north*
Photograph, June 23, 1890
Prints and Photographs Division
Negative LC–USZ62–73552

S14. *View of the west front*
Photograph, May 22, 1891

Prints and Photographs Division
Negative LC–USP6–6512–A

S15. *View of the rear of the building, looking south*
Photograph, March 7, 1892
Prints and Photographs Division
Negative LC–USP6–6611–A

S16. *View of the north front, showing the exterior walls rising at the second floor*
Photograph, April 19, 1893
Prints and Photographs Division
Negative LC–USP6–6518–A

S17. *View of the construction site from the Capitol*
See item 62

S18. *View of the west main pavilion, showing construction of the second floor*
Photograph, June 28, 1892
Prints and Photographs Division
Negative LC–USP6–6628–A

S19. *View of the clerestory arches above the rotunda, with southeast Washington in the distance*
Photograph, June 28, 1892
Prints and Photographs Division
Negative LC–USZ62–73553

S20. *View of the rotunda walls and clerestory windows*
Photograph, September 2, 1892
Prints and Photographs Division
Negative LC–USP6–6517–A

S21. *View of the rotunda rising above the third floor construction work*
Photograph, September 2, 1892
Prints and Photographs Division
Negative LC–USP6–6629–A

S22. *View of the construction site from the Capitol*
See item 66

S23. *View of southwest pavilion and curtain with the rotunda rising above them*
Photograph, November 8, 1892
Prints and Photographs Division
Negative LC–USZ62–73554

S24. *View of interior brickwork in the Main Reading Room*
Photograph, October 14, 1893
Prints and Photographs Division
Negative LC–USZ62–73555

S25. *Brickwork on the first floor of the north curtain*
Photograph, August 8, 1891
Prints and Photographs Division
Negative LC–USZ62–73556

S26. *Floor girders for the Main Reading Room*
Photograph, October 18, 1890
Prints and Photographs Division
Negative LC–USZ62–73557

S27. *Iron framework of the dome's superstructure*
See item 69

S28. *View of the superstructure taking form above the rotunda*
See item 67

S29. *View of southwest pavilion and curtain, with exterior walls completed at the second floor*
Photograph, May 31, 1893
Prints and Photographs Division
Negative LC–USP6–6521–A

S30. *View of the dome during gilding of the lantern*
See item 68

S31. *View of southwest front, with dome covered*
Photograph, November 18, 1893
Prints and Photographs Division
Negative LC–USZ62–73558

S32. *View of the brickwork in the Great Hall*
Photograph, March 19, 1894
Prints and Photographs Division
Negative LC–USP6–6520–A

S33. *View of the Great Hall showing friezes in progress*
Photograph, October 16, 1894

Prints and Photographs Division
Negative LC–USP6–6642–A

S34. *Close view of the west main entrance*
Photograph, December 3, 1891
Prints and Photographs Division
Negative LC–USZ62–73568

S35. *View of west main pavilion stonework*
See item 142

S36. *View of the west facade showing the rotunda's gilded lantern*
See item 70

S37. *View of the west main pavilion from the southwest*
Photograph, May 22, 1895
Prints and Photographs Division
Negative LC–USP6–6525–A

S38. *View of the entrance to the west main pavilion*
Photograph, 1895
Prints and Photographs Division
Negative LC–USP6–6527–A

S39. *View of the west main entrance*
Photograph, May 22, 1895
Prints and Photographs Division
Negative LC–USP6–6526–A

S40. *View of the completed Library of Congress building from the Capitol grounds*
See item 71

Slide Show: Decorating the Building

S41. *Model for bas-relief of "Spring"*
By Bela Lyon Pratt
Photograph, ca. 1895
Prints and Photographs Division
Negative LC–USP6–8694–A

S42. *Completed bas-relief of "Spring"*
By Bela Lyon Pratt
Photograph, ca. 1900
Prints and Photographs Division
Negative LC–USZ6–1096

S43. *Model for bas-relief of "Summer"*
By Bela Lyon Pratt
Photograph, ca. 1895
Prints and Photographs Division
Negative LC–USP6–8693–A

S44. *Completed bas-relief of "Summer"*
By Bela Lyon Pratt
Photograph, ca. 1900
Prints and Photographs Division
Negative LC–USZ6–1097

S45. *Model for bas-relief of "Autumn"*
By Bela Lyon Pratt
Photograph, ca. 1895
Prints and Photographs Division
Negative LC–USP6–6528–A

S46. *Completed bas-relief of "Autumn"*
By Bela Lyon Pratt
Photograph, ca. 1900
Prints and Photographs Division
Negative LC–USZ6–1106

S47. *Model for bas-relief of "Winter"*
By Bela Lyon Pratt
Photograph, ca. 1895
Prints and Photographs Division
Negative LC–USP6–8701–A

S48. *Completed bas-relief of "Winter"*
By Bela Lyon Pratt
Photograph, ca. 1900
Prints and Photographs Division
Negative LC–USZ6–1098

S49. *Bronze sculptures and clock, Main Reading Room*
By John F. Flanagan, with E. Howard Clock &
Watch Company, Boston and New York
Photograph, 1965
Photoduplication Service files

S50. *Plaster sculpture of "Religion" in the Main
Reading Room*
By Theodore Bauer
Photograph, 1966
Photoduplication Service files

S51. *Bronze sculpture of "Moses" before installation*
By Charles Henry Niehaus
Photograph, December 19, 1895
Prints and Photographs Division
Negative LC–USZ6–1099

S52. *Bronze sculpture of "Moses" installed in Main
Reading Room*
By Charles Henry Niehaus
Photograph, 1966
Photoduplication Service files

S53. *Bronze sculpture of "St. Paul" before installation*
By John Donoghue
Photograph, May 2, 1896
Prints and Photographs Division
Negative LC–USZ6–1100

S54. *Bronze sculpture of "St. Paul" installed in the
Main Reading Room*
By John Donoghue
Photograph, 1966
Photoduplication Service files

S55. *Plaster sculpture of "Commerce" before installation*
By John F. Flanagan
Photograph, February 15, 1896
Prints and Photographs Division
Negative LC–USP6–6532–A

S56. *Plaster sculpture of "Commerce" installed in the
Main Reading Room*
By John F. Flanagan
Photograph, 1966
Photoduplication Service files

S57. *Bronze sculpture of "Columbus"*
By Paul Wayland Bartlett
Photograph, 1966
Photoduplication Service files

S58. *Bronze sculpture of "Fulton"*
By Edward Clark Potter
Photograph, 1966
Photoduplication Service files

S59. *Plaster sculpture of "History" in the Main Read-
ing Room*
By Daniel Chester French
Photograph, 1966
Photoduplication Service files

S60. *Bronze sculpture of "Herodotus"*
By Daniel Chester French
Photograph, 1966
Photoduplication Service files

S61. *Bronze sculpture of "Gibbon"*
By Charles Henry Niehaus

Photograph, 1966
Photoduplication Service files

S62. *Plaster sculpture of "Art" in the Main Reading Room*
By François Michel Louis Tonetti-Dozzi after sketches by Augustus St. Gaudens
Photograph, 1966
Photoduplication Service files

S63. *Bronze sculpture of "Michaelangelo"*
By Paul Wayland Bartlett
Photograph, 1966
Photoduplication Service files

S64. *Bronze sculpture of "Beethoven"*
By Theodore Bauer
Photograph, 1966
Photoduplication Service files

S65. *Plaster sculpture of "Philosophy" in the Main Reading Room*
By Bela Lyon Pratt
Photograph, 1966
Photoduplication Service files

S66. *Bronze sculpture of "Plato"*
By John J. Boyle
Photograph, 1966
Photoduplication Service files

S67. *Bronze sculpture of "Bacon"*
By John J. Boyle
Photograph, 1966
Photoduplication Service files

S68. *Plaster sculpture of "Poetry" in the Main Reading Room*
By John Quincy Adams Ward
Photograph, 1966
Photoduplication Service files

S69. *Bronze sculpture of "Homer"*
By Louis St. Gaudens
Photograph, 1966
Photoduplication Service files

S70. *Bronze sculpture of "Shakespeare"*
By Frederick Macmonnies
Photograph, 1966
Photoduplication Service files

S71. *Plaster sculpture of "Law" in the Main Reading Room*
By Paul Wayland Bartlett
Photograph, 1966
Photoduplication Service files

S72. *Bronze sculpture of "Solon"*
By Frederick Wellington Ruckstuhl
Photograph, 1966
Photoduplication Service files

S73. *Bronze sculpture of "Kent"*
By George Edwin Bissell
Photograph, 1966
Photoduplication Service files

S74. *Plaster sculpture of "Science" before installation*
By John Donoghue
Photograph, ca. mid-1895
Prints and Photographs Division
Negative LC–USZ6–1095

S75. *Plaster sculpture of "Science" in the Main Reading Room*
By John Donoghue
Photograph, 1966
Photoduplication Service files

S76. *Bronze sculpture of "Newton"*
By Cyrus Edwin Dallin
Photograph, 1966
Photoduplication Service files

S77. *Bronze sculpture of "Henry"*
By Herbert Adams
Photograph, 1966
Photoduplication Service files

S78. *"Government"*
See item 144

S79. *"Corrupt Legislation"*
See item 145

S80. *"Anarchy"*
See item 148

S81. *"Good Administration"*
See item 153

S82. *"Peace and Prosperity"*
See item 155

S83. *"The Cairn"*
Mural by John White Alexander
Photograph, ca. 1945
Photoduplication Service files

S84. *"Oral Tradition"*
Mural by John White Alexander
Photograph, ca. 1945
Photoduplication Service files

S85. *"Egyptian Hieroglyphics"*
Mural by John White Alexander
Photograph, ca. 1945
Photoduplication Service files

S86. *"Picture Writing"*
Mural by John White Alexander
Photograph, ca. 1945
Photoduplication Service files

S87. *"The Manuscript Book"*
Mural by John White Alexander
Photograph, ca. 1945
Photoduplication Service files

S88. *"The Printing Press"*
Mural by John White Alexander
Photograph, ca. 1945
Photoduplication Service files

S89. *"Melpomene"*
See item 159

S90. *"Clio"*
See item 160

S91. *"Thalia"*
See item 161

S92. *"Euterpe"*
See item 162

S93. *"Terpsichore"*
See item 163

S94. *"Erato"*
See item 164

S95. *"Polyhymnia"*
See item 165

S96. *"Urania"*
See item 166

S97. *"Calliope"*
See item 167

S98. *"Paris"*
See item 168

S99. *"Jason"*
See item 169

S100. *"Bellerophon"*
See item 170

S101. *"Orpheus"*
See item 171

S102. *"Perseus"*
See item 172

S103. *"Prometheus"*
See item 173

S104. *"Theseus"*
See item 174

S105. *"Achilles"*
See item 175

S106. *"Hercules"*
See item 176

S107. *"The Family"*
See item 177

S108. *"Religion"*
See item 178

S109. *"Labor"*
See item 179

S110. *"Study"*
See item 180

S111. *"Rest"*
See item 181

S112. *"Recreation"*
See item 182

S113. *"Instruction"*
See item 183

S114. *"Lyric Poetry"*
See item 184

S115. *"Ganymede"*
See item 185

S116. *"Endymion"*
See item 186

S117. *"Boy of Winander"*
See item 187

S118. *"Uriel"*
See item 188

S119. *"Comus"*
See item 189

S120. *"Adonis"*
See item 190

S121. *"The Poets"*
See item 191

S122. *"Wisdom"*
Mural by Robert Reid
Photograph, 1966
Photoduplication Service files

S123. *"Understanding"*
Mural by Robert Reid
Photograph, 1966
Photoduplication Service files

S124. *"Knowledge"*
Mural by Robert Reid
Photograph, 1966
Photoduplication Service files

S125. *"Philosophy"*
Mural by Robert Reid
Photograph, 1966
Photoduplication Service files

S126. *"Taste"*
Mural by Robert Reid
Photograph, 1966
Photoduplication Service files

S127. *"Sight"*
Mural by Robert Reid
Photograph, 1966
Photoduplication Service files

S128. *"Smell"*
Mural by Robert Reid
Photograph, 1966
Photoduplication Service files

S129. *"Hearing"*
Mural by Robert Reid
Photograph, 1966
Photoduplication Service files

S130. *"Touch"*
Mural by Robert Reid
Photograph, 1966
Photoduplication Service files

S131. *"Spring"*
Mural by Frank Weston Benson
Photograph, 1966
Photoduplication Service files

S132. *"Summer"*
Mural by Frank Weston Benson
Photograph, 1966
Photoduplication Service files

S133. *"Autumn"*
Mural by Frank Weston Benson
Photograph, 1966
Photoduplication Service files

S134. *"Winter"*
Mural by Frank Weston Benson
Photograph, 1966
Photoduplication Service files

S135. *"Aglaia"*
Mural by Frank Weston Benson
Photograph, 1966
Photoduplication Service files

S136. *"Thalia"*
Mural by Frank Weston Benson
Photograph, 1966
Photoduplication Service files

S137. *"Euphrosyne"*
Mural by Frank Weston Benson
Photograph, 1966
Photoduplication Service files

S138. *"War"*
See item 216

S139. *"Peace"*
See item 217

S140. *"The Arts"*
See item 218

S141. *"The Sciences"*
See item 222

S142. *Ceiling mural in the northeast pavilion*
By Elmer Ellsworth Garnsey
Photograph, 1967
Photoduplication Service files

S143. *The Departments of the Treasury and of State*
See item 228

S144. *The Departments of Agriculture and of the Interior*
See item 229

S145. *The Departments of Justice and of the Post Office*
See item 230

S146. *The Departments of War and of the Navy*
See item 231

S147. *Ceiling mural in the northwest pavilion*
By William de Leftwich Dodge
Photograph, 1967
Photoduplication Service files

S148. *"Science"*
See item 232

S149. *"Music"*
See item 233

S150. *"Art"*
See item 234

S151. *"Literature"*
See item 235

S152. *Ceiling mural of the southeast pavilion*
By Elmer Ellsworth Garnsey and Robert L. Dodge
Photograph, undated
Photoduplication Service files

S153. *"Earth"*
See item 236

S154. *"Fire"*
See item 237

S155. *"Water"*
See item 238

S156. *"Air"*
See item 239

S157. *Ceiling mural in the southwest pavilion*
By George Willoughby Maynard
Photograph, 1967
Photoduplication Service files

S158. *"Adventure"*
See item 240

S159. *"Discovery"*
See item 241

S160. *"Conquest"*
See item 242

S161. *"Civilization"*
See item 243

S162. *"The Minerva of Peace"*
See item 245

S163. *View of mosaics in vaulted ceilings, east side, Great Hall, leading to Main Reading Room*
See item 246

S164. *View of mosaics in vaulted ceilings, east side, Great Hall*
See item 247

S165. *View of mosaics in vaulted ceilings, south side, Great Hall*
Color print, Detroit Publishing Company, 1898
Prints and Photographs Division

S166. *"Law" installed above mantel in House Reading Room*
Mosaic by Frederick Dielman
Photograph from MONOGRAPHS OF AMERICAN ARCHITECTURE, vol. 6 (Boston, Ticknor, 1898)
Prints and Photographs Division
Negative LC–USZ62–47266

S167. *"History" installed above mantel in House Reading Room*
Mosaic by Frederick Dielman
Photograph, ca. 1900
Prints and Photographs Division
Negative LC–USZ62–23447

Acknowledgments

An exhibition of this magnitude depends on the cooperation and generosity of a great many individuals and institutions. In particular I would like to thank our colleagues in other institutions who have contributed time, advice, and materials to this exhibition: John H. Dryfhout, Superintendent of the Saint-Gaudens National Historic Site, Windsor, Vermont, National Park Service, U.S. Department of the Interior; Claire A. Stein, National Sculpture Society, New York City; Katherine Kovacs, Archives, Corcoran Gallery of Art, and Laurie Stovall of the Corcoran School of Art; and Ronald E. Swerczek, Diplomatic Branch, National Archives and Records Service. At the Smithsonian Institution the following individuals deserve thanks: Ann Ferrante, Archives of American Art; William A. Stapp, Wendy C. Wick, Barbara A. Bither, Mona L. Dearborn, and Linda Neumaier, National Portrait Gallery; George Gurney, National Collection of Fine Arts, and Catherine Ratzenberger, Susan Rothwell Gurney, and Colleen Hennessey of the NCFA Library; Edward F. Garner and Paula J. Fleming, Museum of Natural History; and David E. Haberstich, Eugene Ostroff, and Linda L. Benbow, Museum of History and Technology.

For lending souvenirs to this exhibition, thanks are owed to Mrs. Corinne Friedman of San Francisco and Washington, D.C.; Mr. and Mrs. Edgar A. Glick of Reston, Virginia; Mr. and Mrs. Warren R. Johnston of Garrett Park, Maryland; Mr. Eugene V. Muench of Terre Haute, Indiana; and Mr. and Mrs. William R. Nugent of Reston, Virginia.

Several members of the U.S. Congress staff were helpful in research: James R. Ketchum of the Office of the Senate Curator; Florian Thayne, Anne Radice, and Mary C. Long in the Office of the Architect of the Capitol; Pauline Medlin of the Senate Environment and Public Works Committee; and Donald A. Ritchie of the Senate Historical Office.

We are also indebted to Sara Dodge Kimbrough, daughter of painter William de Leftwich Dodge and niece of painter Robert Leftwich Dodge; Robert Martiny of Sunnyside, New York, son of sculptor Philip Martiny; Isabelle K. Savell, who helped the Library to identify the sculptor of the symbolic statue of "Art" as François Michel Louis Tonetti Dozzi; and William H. White of the James T. White & Company, Clifton, New Jersey, publishers of the *National Cyclopedia of American Biography* for their assistance in locating photographs of artists who worked on the building.

But with a few exceptions, it is from the rich collections of the Library of Congress that this extensive exhibition has been drawn with the assistance of staff members in many fields of work. We are grateful to Alan Fern for his cooperation and the loan of his personal collection of photographs of the Library and to Mary C. Lethbridge and the staff of the Information Office for their many hours of research and assistance in the development of this exhibition. Our thanks also to Jerry Lee Kearns, Leroy Bellamy, Mary M. Ison, Bernard F. Reilly, Robert L. Lisbeth, C. Ford Peatross, and Annette Melville in the Prints and Photographs Division; James R. Smart of the Motion Picture, Broadcasting, and Recorded Sound Division; Bernard A. Bernier, Jr., and George H. Caldwell of the Serial and

Government Publications Division; Ruth S. Freitag and Edward S. MacConomy of the Office of the Director for General Reference; Nathan R. Einhorn and Mary B. Smith of the Exchange and Gift Division; John J. McDonough, Jr., and Paul G. Sifton of the Manuscript Division; John Charles Finzi, Director of Collections Development; and John Y. Cole, Executive Director of the Center for the Book.

Not every fact about the Library's monumental building is recorded on paper or on film. In the memories of the Library's retirees—those graduates of a special kind of public service whose interest in their institution never flags—are great treasures of information. To them the curator has turned with queries in this instance as in many others: David Chambers Mearns, Mary M. Rock, Legare H. B. Obear, Alvin W. Kremer, Merton S. Foley, Robert H. Land, and Milton Kaplan.

Finally, very special thanks are owed to my colleagues in the Exhibits Office and the Publishing Office, including Leonard C. Faber, Assistant Exhibits Officer, Ingrid Maar, Coordinator of Exhibitions, Evelyn Sinclair, editor of the catalog, and Dana J. Pratt, Director of Publishing.

Helen-Anne Hilker's research on the history of the Library of Congress building began some twenty years ago, and she returned to the Library to act as curator of this exhibition. The Library of Congress is most fortunate to be able to draw upon the special expertise of Miss Hilker, who knows the history of this Library in a most intimate way.

On behalf of this institution I would like to thank Miss Hilker for preserving the heritage of this great national monument.

J. Michael Carrigan
Exhibits Officer